A BOY'S STORY

A BOY'S STORY

The revelations and wild times
of a young skin

MARTIN KING

MAINSTREAM
PUBLISHING
EDINBURGH AND LONDON

Thanks to the following: my wife Mandy, Kortney and Rory, Martin Knight, John King, Irvine Welsh for their support. Plus a big thank you to everyone who put their hands in their pockets and bought *Hoolifan* and *The Naughty Nineties*.

First published in Great Britain in 2000 by

Mainstream Publishing Company (Edinburgh) Ltd

7 Albany Street, Edinburgh EH1 3UG

ISBN 1 84018 333 0

A catalogue record for this book is available from the British Library

Typeset in Joanna MT

Printed and bound in Great Britain by

Creative Print & Design (Wales) Ltd, Ebbw Vale

Contents

 1 The Lure of the Jack and Danny   7

 2 The Boys at the Baseball Game   27

 3 Fair Dos   47

 4 The Sky Blues, Blues   72

 5 Brass Monkeys   86

 6 The Carrot-Crunchers   92

 7 Marching On Together – Leeds United   107

 8 London Overspill   124

 9 The Long Good Friday   135

10 Swatting the Hornets   144

11 The Irons   155

12 Stoke City   173

13 Play Up, Pompey   181

14 School's Out   193

    Epilogue   208

ONE

The Lure of the Jack and Danny

'Right, then, I'm off,' I announced as I plonked my suitcase on the floor and headed for the front door.

'Hold up. Where are you going? Have you unpacked your case and hung your clothes up? Have you sorted out all your smelly socks and pants and put them in the laundry basket? And before you even think about stepping foot outside this house, I suggest you wipe a wet flannel around your grubby little face.'

But before Mum could finish listing the tasks she wanted me to do after our return from holiday, I was out the door and steaming up the road towards the park. I passed Dave, my next-door neighbour.

'Did you have a nice holiday, Mart?' he called out.

'Yes, smashing, thanks, Dave,' I said, but I didn't have time to stop and chat. I knew my mates would be at the park, and one of the best things about going on holiday as a kid was coming home. A week away and you were convinced you'd missed out on all sorts of things. You even kidded yourself that your mates had missed you. Would they accept you back into the scheme of things?

As I reached the rusty iron gates of the rec I could hear my mates playing football.

'Yesss!'

'Bollocks!'

'That was in!'

'No fucking way, that was a mile over the bar!'

'Half-time!' a voice shouts from the other end of the pitch.

It's amazing these games ever progressed at all – I mean, who was Pete to decide it was half-time? Games finished when it got dark or when people got bored or if your mum and dad turned up and ordered you home. There were no time limits. And there were no goalposts or crossbar – two old jumpers marked the goal area but the crossbar was an imaginary, moveable object. Depending on the goalscorer's position in the pecking order, the bar was anywhere between four and twenty-four feet high. When bored with standing around with their hands down their pants, scratching their sweaty nuts, goalkeepers would suddenly declare, 'Rush goalie!' and charge on to the pitch with the thirty-odd outfield players. The rules were made up as we went along, but the games were more freeflowing and enjoyable than any adult football I played – stopping for a fag or to piss against a tree or chat to some passing girl for ten minutes was frowned upon when you turned out for your local pub side.

'Did you have a good holiday, Kingy?' asked Tony as they all dropped onto the patchy yellow grass where many a local dog had cocked its leg. No one seemed to bother as we lay back in the sun.

'Hayling Island any good?' asked Mickey, his arse balanced precariously on the ball. 'See you got a new Ben Sherman – or is it a Brutus?'

'Fuck off, pal, this is a genuine Ben I'll have you know,' I said, looking down proudly at my new shirt.

'Any crumpet down there?' enquired Tony as thirty-four pairs of eyes waited for my answer. Trust Tony to come straight to the point. He was just like me: he loved talking about girls and chasing them.

I wiggled my eyebrows, Terry Venables style, and waited till I had everyone's attention. 'I did meet one old sort down there,' I told them at last. 'She was well tasty – fifteen years old.'

Her age prompted a gasp from my attentive audience. To twelve- and thirteen-year-olds like us, contact of a sexual nature with a fifteen-year-old girl was as unattainable as it would have been with Valerie Singleton. We had all watched her on TV and dreamt of sticking our tongues down the gorgeous Valerie's throat.

'The girl I met on holiday was tall and slim with a spider-cut hairdo. Oh yeah, I nearly forgot – she had the most beautiful pair of tits I've ever seen in my life. The only trouble is she lives down in Portsmouth.'

'Did you shaft her?' This was from Colin. You got no verbal foreplay with him. Colin was obsessed with sex. Given the choice, some of us were still young enough to choose a game of football over a fumble with a bird. Not Colin, though: he was older than most of us so we all assumed he was knowledgeable in the ways of the world. 'Well, Kingy,' he persisted, 'did ya fuck her or not?'

'I ain't saying,' I replied. 'I promised I'd keep our love life a secret.' I looked down at the ground, feigning embarrassment. After a pause, I continued my fantasy. 'It's funny how we met. I was playing football in a staff versus guests match one afternoon, and before the game kicked off I noticed her standing on the touchline.

'My uncle Jack, who for years had told me what a good footballer he was, lined up alongside me in the guests' team. Jack's tales of how he could have been a pro player were legendary. "I should have played for England," he'd tell me. But war broke out with Germany and he had to go off and serve his country. He claims he turned out for an army side against a Royal Navy eleven, and ended up scoring a hat-trick, and from there he went on to play for a combined forces team against a world eleven where, after scoring a hat-trick in the first half, he was forced to go in goal due to a injury to the keeper. He even saved two penalties. He was carried off on his team-mates' shoulders at the end of the game. He was a real-life Roy of the Rovers.

'Funny thing was, I never even seen him kick a ball. My doubts were soon proved correct when after ninety minutes of play he hadn't touched the ball once. Jack claimed that was because he was played out of position out on the left-wing. We won six-nil, and Jack reckons the reason we won so convincingly was because he had four men marking him all the time, and that gave the rest of the lads more room in which to play.

'When the game finished this girl came over. "You played really well," she said. She told me her name was Teresa and that she had seen me around the camp. I told her my name and asked her if she wanted to meet up later. We met by the pool, and one thing led to another and later on that evening we ended up snogging. She had the softest lips I've ever kissed.'

'And?' said Tony. 'Did she know you were only fourteen?'

'She never asked.'

'Did she give you a hand shandy?' As usual, Colin's imagination was running about ten minutes ahead of the rest of us.

'No. After we snogged I started to tit her up.'

'Inside or outside her top?' asked Peter, stuttering with excitement.

'Inside, of course.' I smiled as if a wonderful memory had flooded back to me.

'Inside or outside her bra?'

I smiled to create the impression it was the former.

'How big were they?'

'Massive,' I said. 'And they were firm like rocks, not soft and saggy like some birds' tits.'

'Did you get them out?' asked Mick as he leaned further and further towards me as the story hotted up. Eventually he was leaning so far forward he slipped off the ball and we all fell about laughing.

'I think she liked the aftershave,' I smiled as I took up the story again. In those days I was practically bathing in Brut. Henry Cooper, the boxer, advertised it on the telly and young skinheads like me bought it by the gallon. 'Splash it all over,' our Henry used to say in the advert. I didn't have a hair on my chin worth shaving but that didn't stop me from getting through at least one of the little green bottles a week. Come to think of it, I didn't have much hair around my bollocks either. I was proud of the few hairs that had grown just below my belly button and made a point of keeping the lower buttons of my shirt undone in the hope that my newly discovered manliness might attract some girl.

'When I told this bird I was one of the Chelsea Shed boys and went with all the top skinhead faces from around the Mitcham area, she became like putty in my hands and she was all over me,' I went on.

'Come on, come on, don't fuck about! Did you shag her or not?' demanded Mick.

'What do you think?' I fired back and at the same time shoved my forefinger under his nose.

He yelled something about the smell being like Billingsgate fish market. 'That's disgusting, Kingy,' said Mick as he walked backwards to get out of my way. 'I don't believe anyone can be that filthy – touch a girl's fanny and then travel halfway across the country without washing their hands.'

I was well pleased. His remarks and actions only added credence to my story – my fingers hadn't been anywhere near a girl's fanny.

At that moment, as if acting on some unspoken command, we all jumped up and took up our positions on the pitch.

'Skins versus shirts!' shouted Tony. 'Get your shirt off, Kingy.'

I wasn't going to risk putting my new Ben Sherman on the grass to have it kicked all over the place and ruined, so I hung my braces down by my sides and tied the shirt around my waist. And there was no way I was going to tackle anyone – I didn't want green stains on my white Sta-prest Levis.

A couple of girls walked past, their transistor radio booming out a reggae beat. The game slowed down as I ran alongside them, dancing in time to the music. It raised a laugh.

'You can get it if you really want,' promised Desmond Dekker as the light started to fade and night-time closed in.

Up went the shout 'Next goal wins'. With the game being a draw at ten goals each, something was needed to break the deadlock. Unfortunately I couldn't recapture my holiday-camp form and Jeff let in a shot from the halfway line when he took his eyes off the game to wind his watch up. Everyone cheered as the winning goal went in, some because their team had been victorious, and others with sheer relief that the game was over at last. Like most of our games, it had dragged on just a little too long.

We gathered up our gear and drifted towards the gates with

Horace, the old park-keeper, bringing up the rear like a sheepdog.

'You scallywags might not have homes to go to,' he mumbled, 'but I certainly have.'

'You'd be lost without us lot to talk to,' I told him.

'You just want to get home and give Mrs Horace a good seeing to,' said Colin, again bringing the conversation round to his favourite subject.

Horace snorted and smiled and said something about thirty years ago maybe. A couple of lads cycled round him on their track bikes, pulling back on the handlebars so just one knobbly tyre was on the ground. They made grunting noises – the sound they imagined Horace made when making love to his wife.

Horace chuckled. We all liked him and didn't really give him any serious gyp. He'd known most of our mums and dads when they were our age. In the winter he always had an old log fire burning in his hut and he would let us sit in there when the weather was at its coldest. Some of the boys ponced roll-ups from him and they would sit talking and smoking together. He could roll a fag with just one hand, spinning the cigarette round with his nicotine-stained fingers with amazing skill. He told us stories of the war – the bombings, gas-masks, ration-books. He saw it as the good old days. He was so old he could remember when Mitcham was a country village.

Two days later a letter arrived on my doormat. I noticed the Portsmouth postmark and immediately tore open the envelope. Inside was a note from Teresa, telling me how much she was missing me. She'd also enclosed a holiday snap of the two of us standing smiling, hand-in-hand, by the pool.

Mum was standing behind me, reading the letter over my shoulder. 'Holiday romances never last,' she said unkindly.

'Well, how come she's invited me down next weekend to see her, then?'

Mum just shook her head and laughed. I had already fantasised about turning up at Teresa's big house overlooking the bay. When I get down there, Mummy and Daddy are out and within minutes

Teresa's drawers are around her ankles and I'm pumping away like a champion. Even in my daydream I peak in seconds.

Mum interrupted. 'Anyway, who do you think is going to take you all the way down to Portsmouth?' Cos me and your dad certainly ain't traipsing up and down the country looking for some young hussy.'

'I'll take myself,' I told her huffily, wondering why Mum was making out I was pursuing some old trout who didn't want to know.

'You will, won't ya. If the school board find out I've let a child of fourteen travel on their own on a train to Portsmouth I'd be locked up for good.'

'Mum, I can get on a train at Wimbledon. I won't have to change and when I get there I'll phone and let you know that I've arrived safely.'

She seemed to be softening a little. She paused a while and then said, 'How do you know they'll even have a phone?'

'Most people have a phone nowadays,' I told her. 'Anyway, she says she's going to ring me this Thursday at seven to see if I'm going.'

We hadn't had a phone very long. Mum liked to think that we were special and had something the rest of the population didn't. She went quiet again and I knew if she said 'Ask your father' I'd cracked it.

'What about if you have one of your turns in someone else's house? You know what you're like, son,' she said at last. 'I don't think her mum and dad will be best pleased if you turn up stark bollock naked at the end of their bed in the middle of the night.'

She had a point. I was going through a serious sleepwalking phase.

'I'll just go down for the day, then.'

'That'll be nice,' grinned Mum.

I decided to ask a couple of the boys to go with me. Teresa was bound to have a few mates, I reckoned, and when they clocked us in our Prince of Wales check trousers, Harrington jackets, Fred Perry's and wet-look Gibson shoes, they'd be bowled over by our clobber. I doubted they'd ever seen a pair of tonics in Portsmouth. Probably still got Teddy boys down there, I told myself.

Sure enough, just after seven on Thursday the phone rang. Mum and Dad were watching *Tomorrow's World*, the programme people tolerated while waiting for *Top of the Pops* to come on.

'What a load of shit this is,' Mum was saying. She and I both jumped up and headed for the ringing phone in the hallway. 'That'll be for me,' she proclaimed.

'It's for me,' I said. I got to the blower first but a swift elbow in the ribs from Mum sent me sprawling on the floor.

'Hello, Six-Four-Eight-Oh-Two-Four-Nine. Mrs King here. To whom am I speaking?' she demanded in her best Lady Penelope voice. Owning a telephone had had a strange effect on my mother. As well as the new voice, she always stood erect with a fixed smile on her face when talking. She even fiddled with her hair as if the person on the other end of the line could see her.

I could hear Teresa ask sweetly if she could talk to me.

'Mart, phonecall for you. I think it's that little tart from Hayling Island,' Mum laughed as she handed the receiver to me.

'*You fucking wait*,' I mouthed but she just laughed as she stuck two fingers up at me and went back to join Dad in the front room.

'Excuse my mother, Teresa, she's got a warped sense of humour. How are you?' I said.

'I'm great. How are you?' she giggled nervously.

'I'm fine, it's lovely to hear from you.' I was so excited I wasn't sure what to say.

'I just rang to see if you got my letter and if you could come down here one weekend. It would be so lovely to see you. I miss you so much. I've even written your name on the cover of my English exercise book at school.'

'Yeah, I'd love to come down,' I replied. 'Which weekend did you have in mind? Trouble is, I go to watch Chelsea most weekends.'

'Oh,' she said, sounding disappointed.

'But I'd give up watching Chelsea to be with you.' That statement made even me cringe, and I could feel my face going red. From the other end of the hall I could hear the splutter of muffled laughter. I quietly asked Teresa to hold the line and carried on talking aloud as I tiptoed up the hall to the kitchen door and pushed it open. Standing there was my mother.

'All right, Ma,' I said. 'Having a good old listen, are we?'

She went straight on the defensive. 'I ain't earwigging your small talk if that's what you think.'

'So why have you got your ear pressed up against the door?'

'Oh, fuck off,' she growled. That was Mum's answer to everything.

I went back to chatting to Teresa. I told her I was thinking of bringing a few mates down with me and she said she thought it was a good idea. We scheduled my visit for a week on Saturday.

'I've told all my friends about you, Martin, and how you're one of the leaders of the Chelsea Shed.'

'Did I really tell you that?'

'I told the boy who lives next door to me that you're a proper London skinhead,' she went on, 'and he said that the Chelsea Shed are nothing, and that they wouldn't dare show their faces in Portsmouth.'

'Listen, Teresa, you tell that wanker of a next-door neighbour that Chelsea don't run from anyone, and if I ever meet him I'll knock him spark out, the wanker,' I said, getting angry.

'I don't really see a lot of him,' she admitted. 'He's a scaffolder and he works away from home a lot of the time.'

'How old is he, then?' I said after a pause.

'He's about nineteen,' replied Teresa. 'Next time I see him – he's usually in the back garden working out with his weightlifting gear – I'll pass on your message.'

'Don't worry. I'll tell him myself if I see him.'

Me and my big mouth! Here I am, five foot nothing and six stone of hot air and piss, and I'm throwing down the gauntlet to some hairy-arsed construction worker.

The next day, I told Jeff and Tony about the plans I'd made on their behalf. I had toyed with the idea of inviting Colin but the thought of him alighting from the train at Portsmouth and immediately grabbing the breasts of Teresa's best friend persuaded me it wouldn't be a good idea.

'Great,' purred Tony. 'D'you reckon we'll be on for a shag or even a wank?' Tony was already lowering his expectations.

Jeff didn't say too much, but Jeff didn't have a lot to say at the best of times. He was the mean and moody one. He was a couple of years older than me, so perhaps he'd seen it all before. Funny, though, I don't remember ever seeing him with a bird. His idea of fun was climbing up a high wall or onto a factory roof that no one else would have the bottle to attempt. But he was a sound bloke and everyone liked him. My mum was fond of him because she said he was always polite when he came to our house and always looked clean and tidy.

During the week we met up to pinch the empty lemonade bottles from the back of the local off-licence. They were worth quite a bit of money. This raid was carried out under cover of darkness. It meant crossing the locked park without being spotted and clearing the fence at the back of the shop where the empty bottles were stacked in crates. This had to be done as quietly as possible.

'Wait!' said Tony stopping in his tracks. 'There's something up near the back of the shop.'

We could just make out a shape heading in our direction. Was it the owner lying in wait with the Old Bill? Did we give ourselves up or run like the clappers? We did neither. The mystery shape turned out to be the shopkeeper's dog, Prince, his tail wagging nine to the dozen when he realised it was us. We bent down to say hello to him and he gave our faces a good licking with his big pink wet tongue. He knew us well – we were in the shop most days – and we always said hello to him and gave him lots of fuss.

'He knows our smell – dogs have a good sense of smell,' said Jeff.

'He must be good with disguises – I've just farted,' said Tony. 'I hope Teresa's mates' breath doesn't smell like that,' he went on, wiping Prince's slobber from his cheeks.

We all started giggling which soon turned into fits of loud laughter.

'Don't fuck about,' I said eventually. We grabbed a crate each and clambered back over the fence and headed down the road to another off-licence, where we got two pence for each empty bottle, no questions asked.

All we could talk about that week was the excursion. It was already taking on the allure of some kind of life-changing adventure. Some of the other boys wanted to tag along but I knew too many representatives of CFC and the south London skins would certainly reduce the chances of success in the Jack and Danny stakes.

The night before the big day we made the final arrangements as the evening's football marathon drew to an end at the park. Jeff and Tony were to call for me at eight o'clock the next morning, and I told Teresa we would meet her and her mates at eleven at Portsmouth Harbour station. The rest of the boys wished us luck and told us they'd be smelling our fingers when we returned.

I decided to have an early night – I'd a busy day ahead and needed to save my energy for all that shagging I was going to be doing. At the top of the road I caught up with my dad who was leisurely riding his bike home from a long day at work. He got off and walked alongside me. 'How's it going, boy?'

'Dad, I've been meaning to ask you something.'

'If it's about your trip to Portsmouth to see that girl, save your breath – your mother's already told me. You can go, but behave yourself and don't get into any bother.'

'Cheers, Dad.' I was genuinely surprised that Mum and Dad still had conversations after nearly twenty years of marriage.

When we reached the house Dad lifted the bike over the front doorstep and pushed it into the hallway. As he bent down to remove his bicycle clips, I asked him why he didn't leave the bike in the garden.

'Oh, yeah, so one of your mates or some other arsehole can half-inch it? Thirty years ago, maybe, when I was a kid, you could leave your front door unlocked, and nothing ever got nicked, but now –' he stopped.

'Do you think that may have had something to do with the fact that years ago you had nothing worth pinching?' I countered cheekily.

'Your sauce will be the death of you one day, son.'

Mum liked Fridays even more than I did because once the old man was home from work and had hung his coat up in the hallway, he would hand over his unopened wage packet. Mum would tear open the brown envelope with Dad's name written on it and count out some notes which she would place in the front pocket of the flowered apron around her waist. The rest of the money, still inside the brown envelope, was stuffed inside an old tea-pot. I swore blind that if ever I got married there was no way I'd hand over my hard-earned cash that easily. I suppose Dad saw it as the only way to a quiet life. He would sink into his favourite armchair and Mum would place his dinner tray on his lap.

That was normally our signal to charge off to the corner shop and have a spending spree, topping up on everything that had run low during the week and doing the bulk of the main shopping the next day. An ounce of golden Virginia for Dad, sixty tipped fags for the old girl, and for me a bottle of Tizer or Cream Soda, some black licorice and sherbert flying saucers, plus a football magazine – something like *Shoot!* or *Goal*.

Back at the house I'd devour the mag almost as quickly as the sweets and before you knew it I'd have ripped out the centre pages and any colour pictures of Chelsea players to be stuck on my bedroom wall with small pieces of sellotape beside the hundreds of other football pictures I had. Players I didn't like from other teams would have beards, glasses and moustaches drawn on them with pen.

'You wasteful little git, I've just paid two bob for that!' Mum would shout with traces of chocolate round her lips.

Saturday morning, and I was up with the lark. Mum and Dad were awake already. I could hear the sound of chinking cups and the kettle boiling. The radio was on and the drone of Ed Stewart's voice was drifting from the kitchen. I set about choosing something to wear. I decided on my red-and-blue checked short-sleeved Ben Sherman shirt and my white Levis Sta-prest which Mum had ironed the night before. The trouser legs were turned up so far you could see the whole of my polished ox-blood-coloured Dr Marten boots. 'If you have them bleedin' trousers any further up your leg, people will think you've got Bermuda shorts on,' Dad always used to say.

Putting those boots on was a big part of being a skinhead. There was no doubt about it: when you had them on you felt better equipped to deal with life on the streets. They made you feel ten times harder and meaner. I'm sure most skinheads felt the same way.

I pulled on my deep-blue Harrington jacket and slipped my long steel comb into the inside pocket, not for combing my hair – I didn't have any – but for protection. I'd heard the older boys say they carried them in case of trouble or, God forbid, if someone screwed at them. Screwing was the main source of communication among the different gangs of skins. Seeing I was going on a mission deep into unknown territory, I knew I'd feel safer with one stuck in my pocket, though if someone started on me I'd be more likely to give them a rotten hairdo than maim them. For a finishing touch I rubbed some Brut into my neck and chest and behind my ears.

The doorbell rang and I heard Mum say hello to Jeff and Tony. 'You two silly bastards on the crumpet trail too?'

My mates never knew how to take my mum, but out of respect for an adult, they never took her piss-taking and joking seriously. They never said much back.

As I came down the stairs we weighed each other up. Jeff had on a white Fred Perry with mint-coloured Sta-prest and you could see your face in the shine of his polished fringe-and-buckle loafers. Tony was wearing his green Harrington over a Jamaican check Brutus shirt and a pair of Levi's jeans, the legs rolled up nearly to his knees, and his eighteen-hole DMs. We all had cropped hair courtesy of Peter

Marney's father, Eddie. He ran a little barber's shop in Bond Road and he'd crop your hair any way you wanted. He'd cut it to a 64th of an inch, a 32nd, a 16th, an 8th, a quarter or a half inch. Most of the kids opted for the latter two. A couple of boys turned up at school one morning with a 64th. The headmistress sent them home until their hair had grown back to what she deemed an acceptable length.

We strode off towards the station, nervous and at the same time excited about the adventure that lay ahead. Even thinking about the journey gave me a buzz. It's strange how everything seems to be so much further away when you're that age. A trip sixty miles to the coast was a huge event that had taken us days of planning. Now people commute that far to work every day and no one gives it a second thought. When I was fourteen, if you had relatives who lived over sixty miles away you'd be lucky to see them from one year to the next. Not many people owned a car, so until the telephone became widely affordable to the working classes, having cousins in darkest Devon was little different to having relatives in Australia.

As the pace picked up in our eagerness to meet the girls, I was a shade worried that Teresa might innocently let it be known to the others that, far from shagging her on holiday, I had in fact been nowhere near her. All right, we had kissed, and maybe my hand had accidentally brushed against her tits, but if the truth came out I'd never live it down. As we passed Fry's Metals where Dad worked and headed over the bridge and down towards Colliers Wood Station, the conversation between me and Tony centred around hands down drawers, lovebites, where we should buy our Johnnie bags (Durex) and whether we should consider swapping partners when we got bored.

Jeff didn't join in and was just walking along smiling to himself. Eventually he spoke. 'Martin, fuck the girls.'

'I certainly hope so, Jeff.'

'No, I mean, fuck them as in forget them. Let's go up to West Bromwich and watch Chelsea play. We've got the money and we're out for the day.'

'Where the fuck's West Brom?' Tony and I said in unison. I knew they were in the First Division, had Jeff Astle playing for them and had beaten Everton in the Cup final recently, but my knowledge of them ended there.

'It's only the other side of Birmingham,' Jeff told us. 'Look, you two have never been to a Chelsea game outside of London – now's your chance. Just think what all the other kids will say when they hear you're part of the Chelsea away-day crew.'

Tony and I looked at one another and then at Jeff.

'I've heard there's going to be a mass bundle up there today and Greenaway wants everyone to turn up,' Jeff went on.

The thought of Greenaway, this famous mystical figure, wanting me to stand next to him as we went into battle convinced me I had to be there. That did the trick and I'm sure that was Jeff's intention.

'Yeah, let's go up there,' I said.

Tony looked at me as if I'd lost the plot and mumbled something about never meeting a bit of minge, but then he nodded his head in agreement.

We hadn't even reached the station and we'd gone from fanny-chasing in Portsmouth to leading the Chelsea Shed into battle nearly two hundred miles north. Once on the train, we realised that our tube wouldn't take us all the way to the Midlands and that we'd have to change somewhere.

'It'll be King's Cross, St Pancras or Euston,' said Jeff as he ran his finger along the map of the underground, standing on his seat to reach it. A kid, probably a couple of years younger than me sitting opposite us with his dad, pointed out that to get to Birmingham we would need to change at Euston. They were both decked out in blue-and-white scarves and bobble hats. I started chatting to them about the team and how they thought today's game might go and where Birmingham was. Jeff shot me a disapproving look.

When we came out onto the vast Euston concourse he told me to hurry up. 'We don't want to be seen with them dingbats.'

There were groups of Chelsea fans dotted all over the station and when the BR announcer said the next train for Birmingham New Street Station would depart from Platform 1, all the Chelsea boys made their way to the train. Once on board, we roamed up and down looking for seats. It was a bit disappointing – no Greenaway or Eccles or any of the other famous faces from the Shed. There didn't even seem to be anyone who looked up for a fight.

'The chaps must have been on a earlier train,' offered Jeff. It suddenly struck me that I'd dropped a bollock. I could have been down in Portsmouth right now, my tongue tickling Teresa's tonsils and my hand foraging inside her bra. Instead, here I was, bound for a place I'd hardly heard of, miles further than I'd ever been before in my life without Mum or Dad knowing or agreeing, with who-knows-what waiting at our destination. I was scared and gutted at the same time. I didn't tell Jeff and Tony but I decided I was going to jump off the train before it left Euston and head to Portsmouth. But, as John Lennon once said, life is what happens when you're busy making other plans: the train chugged into life and it felt like the course of my life might be about to change for ever.

For a good ten minutes no one said a word. I just looked out the window, furious with myself. How could I be so fucking stupid? I'd been tricked into doing something I didn't want to do. What made it worse was that it was someone I had a lot of time for who had conned me.

Two older boys I knew from school came along the train and sat down beside us. I started to feel a bit better. They told us that a train had left Euston half an hour before this one with about five hundred Chelsea boys on board. The only reason they themselves hadn't caught that one was because they were dodging the fare and there were too many ticket inspectors hanging around the departure gate.

'How do you get through at the other end?' I asked.

'Piece of piss. When we get to the other end we look for an old lady and ask her if she would like a hand with her bags. Nine times out of ten, they say, "Yes, please, oh, how kind of you to offer, young man." Then we walk through the ticket barrier in front of her, nod backwards at the old girl and say, "My nan's got the tickets," to the man on the gate. When we're safely through, we drop the bags and run. Works every time,' they said.

'This is great,' I thought. It sounded worth the price of the train ticket just to see this crack.

When the train pulled in at Birmingham New Street station, the five of us jumped off and took a local train to West Smethwick. When we spotted the floodlights out the window it was like finding the promised land.

'There's the ground! That's the Hawthorns!' gasped one of the woolly-hat brigade and we all pushed our faces up against the glass in awe.

We got off the train and set off for the stadium. The area around the station looked like it had been bombed during the war and no one could be bothered to rebuild it. We had to cross a stretch of wasteland to reach the stadium, which was about half a mile away. Half walking, half running, we led our motley mixture of fans forward.

Up ahead, loitering in the distance, was a group of boys. As we got closer I could see they were a couple of years older than us. They were not from London – I could tell that by the way they were dressed. The biggest one in the gang really fancied himself and was giving us the eye. He looked like an unwashed Cliff Richard from the film *Summer Holiday*, all brylcreemed black hair, shirt open to the waist and ripped jeans covered in oil stains. The others were a right scruffy bunch of wankers, I thought, in their leather jackets and winklepicker boots.

Jeff was the first to react. He bent down and picked up a four-foot-long piece of timber. The two boys we'd met on the train rolled up the sleeves of their Harrington jackets and stood alongside him. 'Come on, you northern arseholes, we're ready!' one of them called.

Jeff might have been, but I wasn't so sure. Fortunately, the Elvis fan club didn't fancy it and ran off towards the stadium, shouting insults over their shoulders.

'Charge!' yelled one of the anoraks and everyone gave chase.

Clouds of dust rose into the air as hundreds of people stampeded across the rubble-strewn wasteland.

I couldn't believe it! Here we were on our first trip out of London, and when trouble comes along, we're right in the front line!

By the time we reached the stadium it sounded from the noise coming from inside that the game had already kicked off. We found the away supporters' entrance and got in, taking up a position behind the goal. The Chelsea fans had nearly filled the whole of our allocated terrace. It was a great feeling to be so far from home surrounded by thousands of your own.

Huddled in intense conversation round a tea stall was a group of twenty guys I recognised immediately. None of them seemed to be paying any attention to the match. I edged closer. I could hear one man talking and everyone else listening. 'We should be in there!' he shouted, pointing towards the huge home end at the far side of the ground. 'Not in here! We should be showing that West Brom lot that we're Chelsea!'

It was Eccles. I'd run into him a couple of times but had not yet made his acquaintance, though I was determined to sooner or later. He wore a black Fred Perry with the gold motif, and his muscles positively bulged out of the sleeves. His torso looked rock solid. His face was set in grim determination. He was by no means the biggest bloke there, but charisma positively oozed from him.

As I listened to their post-match plans Teresa suddenly popped back into my head. I imagined we were under the pier (I reckoned there must be one near where she lived – it was the coast, after all) and she was groaning with pleasure as my hand explored inside her lace bra and then slid all the way down her body before stopping at her fanny. 'Take me, Martin, take me,' she groaned.

'Come on, Kingy, stop daydreaming, we're on the move.' The game had ended and Jeff was telling me to keep up with him. A sea of Harrington jackets and cropped hair swept down the terraces and out onto the street. Most turned left towards the wasteground and the station but I had my eye firmly fixed on Eccles and company, who turned right out of the ground and headed towards the home end. We came to a main road at the back of the stadium. Everyone stopped. Thousands of West Brom fans were streaming past us. A fish-and-chip shop was doing brisk business with hundreds of people queuing to get inside. A pub which hadn't yet opened had hordes of people milling about outside. All eyes turned to us and the cry of '*Albion, Albion, Albion!*' filled the street.

'*Chelsea, Chelsea!*' we chanted in response. Suddenly the Albion fans' urge for beer and chips subsided and they cleared the streets. We hadn't even run at them! We gave chase to a few stragglers, running after them for what seemed like miles. It was great fun and I didn't see anyone get hurt.

Finally, Eccles stopped and so everyone else did too. 'That'll do,' he laughed. It was the first time I'd ever seen him smile.

'Those northerners won't forget us in a hurry,' volunteered a boy not much older than me.

Eccles turned around and gave him a long hard stare. The smile was gone and he spoke through gritted teeth. 'Birmingham are only up the road and they've always given us a good row, so don't give it all that old bollocks about northerners.'

I wondered why Eccles said that. How come Birmingham City got respect and West Bromwich didn't when both clubs pulled their support from the same area? This football thing was beginning to fascinate me.

As we walked back to the station we would have ripped the dark-blue-and-white scarves from the necks of any West Brom fans we came across. This was common practice for a few years, like Red Indians collecting their victims' scalps. Some were even loosening their scarves as we approached, handing them over as a sort of peace offering. This was my first experience of the awe and fear with which northern football supporters regarded Chelsea. Our reputation had definitely gone before us. All the talk I'd heard on the Stamford Bridge terraces about the Chelsea boys' exploits outside London looked from today's evidence to be true. The feeling of pride was hard to explain, but for a couple of hours we – a bunch of two-bob wannabe skins from Mitcham – were powerful, frightening and admired. Or so we thought.

I arrived back home just as the opening bars of the *Match of the Day* theme tune blared out from the telly.

'Before you take your coat off and sit down, boy, do you think you can adjust that poxy aerial? There's been a shadow on that screen all night and it's getting right on my bleedin' nerves,' said Mum, pushing the last of her fish supper down her throat.

'All right, son, had a good day with your lady friend?' smiled Dad.

'Hope you ain't brought no VD into this house,' grinned Mum.

I tossed my crumpled West Brom programme on to the table.

'You been up there, then, boy?' asked the old man like he was pleasantly surprised I'd chosen football over girls. He flicked through the programme as I leant back in the armchair and fell asleep as a mixture of the day's events and Kenneth Wolstenholme's droning voice took effect.

A few days later I was lying on my bed thinking of Teresa and what might have been when Mum burst through the door brandishing a letter. 'I think this is from that girl.'

'You know the letter's from Teresa because you've been nosy and read what she's sent me.'

'No, I ain't – it's probably that bastard postman who's opened it.'

'Oh yeah, I'm sure he's interested in my private life.' I glared at the old girl and then read the letter as Mum watched for my reaction.

Teresa said that she and her mates had waited at the station until six in the evening. How could I make such a fool of her in front of her mates? She realised now that I'd been leading her on all the time, and she hoped she would never set eyes on me again. In her words she had been utterly humiliated. I felt terrible.

Mum couldn't hide her glee. 'I told ya, boy, that holiday romances never last,' she laughed as she turned and walked out of the room.

TWO

The Boys at the Baseball Game

Our visit to the Hawthorns certainly whetted my appetite for Chelsea away games. Because I was still at school, though, it was difficult to fund such trips on the loose change given to me by my dad or brother, especially when I was also trying to keep up with the ever-changing face of fashion. I had to take on part-time jobs – as many as I could physically manage. But being only five foot tall and weighing in at just six stone, I needed most of my energy for the local girls.

The newsagent on the corner of our street gave me a Monday-to-Saturday paper-round for which I got the princely sum of £1.50. I also did a Sunday round that earned me another 60p – or twelve bob in old money. (My mum was the worst when it came to converting the old pounds, shillings and pence into what she called 'this new-fangled money'. I hated going shopping with her when decimalisation came in. 'What's that in real money?' she would ask the shop-keeper, giving them a look as if to say, 'I know you're conning me, you swindling bastard.')

My Sunday round was very quiet and I hardly saw a soul out early in the mornings. I'd just stroll round, reading all the football reports in the papers I had to deliver. From Monday to Friday, I'd come across early-risers off to work, people walking their dogs, keep-fit fanatics out running and weirdos hanging around in the shadows. In the winter, when it was cold and dark, it was especially eerie, and whenever someone came towards me I'd brace myself for an attack. As they drew level I'd try to remember what Batman and Robin had done when they had a run-in with The Riddler or The Penguin.

'Cold enough for you, son?' or 'Morning, boy,' most of them said, and they'd walk past smiling. Only then did I relax. I don't know how paper-boys and girls these days cope with those huge Sunday papers containing fifty-seven sections and countless colour supplements – how do you get something that bulky through the letterbox? I don't think any of my customers read the posh broadsheets – it was mainly the News of the World, The People and the Sunday Mirror.

Some weekends I also helped the milkman. My mate Jack Wright used to do the round but he gave it up and let me do it when he got a new job delivering bread door to door. The milkman used to bung me a quid for helping him. I basically did his job – he definitely got top value for money. I would run up and down the garden paths delivering the milk and taking away the empties. All he had to do was release the handbrake on the float and follow me as I hurried between houses. Now and then he would rise from his semi-slumber, gather up his leather moneybag and big book, and disappear inside a house for half an hour. He always came out doing up his flies and flattening his hair down, with some right dollybird standing at her door in a see-through nightie blowing him a kiss goodbye.

'How long have you been wearing lipstick?' I used to ask him. 'I hope the wife doesn't spot that on the collar of your shirt when you get home.' I enjoyed tormenting the life out of him, the lazy bastard.

So if I was lucky, I could end up with £3.60 by the weekend. And, with my well-earned wedge in my pocket, I'd be straight down to Tooting Broadway on my weekly tour of the menswear shops. Most times I'd go home with something new. There was always something that would catch my eye and I'd promise to treat myself to it the following week. Top of the list of clothes to get were Ben Sherman shirts (£2.50), Brutus and Jaytex shirts (£1.50), which were similar in style to a Ben with their buttondown collar, pleat and hook and nice checks. They didn't have quite the same street cred, though, and were a bit of a poor cousin. Levi's Sta-prest trousers were £4, and the in colours were white (the skins' favourite), mint green, sky blue, navy, black (for school) and bottle green. A Harrington jacket would set you back £3 and a pair of the good doctor's boots a mere fiver. For those with a bit of extra cash and anyone who wanted to look a bit flash, a sleeveless jumper at only £2 would finish your wardrobe off nicely.

Occasionally the old man would take me up to Petticoat Lane over in the east end of London. It was the Mecca of fashion for all serious skinheads. I knew if my dad was taking me there, some serious money was going to be spent. One particular Sunday morning he ended up buying me a crombie overcoat from this little Jewish old boy who ran a stall there. The coat set Dad back £8 and I felt like a millionaire in it. I told him I'd wear it home. I was as pleased as punch and as I walked through the crowded market I kept looking down at myself and in every shop window to try to get a look at my reflection.

It was a different story when we got home, though. Mum's biting wit soon brought me back down to earth. 'Fucking hell, Fred, did you find this little Jewish boy outside an East End synagogue,' she said as she looked at me, pissing herself with laughter.

The next day I went to a clothes shop in the centre of Mitcham and bought a red silk handkerchief. I fixed it with a gold stud so that it hung from the top pocket of my crombie. It was the perfect finishing touch. It's amazing how clothes can transform you – or I should say it's amazing how you *think* clothes can transform you. Once I put on that crombie I felt different. I was more *adult*. I was better-looking. I was a better fighter. I commanded more respect. I was *numero uno*. The coat's long sleeves came down nearly to my fingertips – it was miles too big for me. I expect Dad noticed that when I was trying it on but decided to keep quiet so that I'd get a few extra months' wear out of it. He knew I'd grow out of things at a very rapid rate. One minute you're Charlie Drake and the next you're bigger than a Harlem Globe Trotter. No wonder the old girl chuckled at me. I could have begun a career as a magician there and then – it would have been a great coat for hiding packs of cards, rabbits and white doves.

Worn on top of my two-tone red-and-blue mohair suit, bought

on a recent shopping expedition with the old man in Croydon, the crombie really increased my marketability among the local girls, even though it was a touch on the warm side when worn on a hot summer's day. Still, the weather shouldn't come into it when you're a serious poseur.

The real difficulty was choosing which shoes to wear with my Sunday best: the slip-on leather loafers with the fringed tassles or the box Gibsons with the wet-look finish, the ones that looked like you'd pissed over them by mistake? Or there were the Ivy brogues or the Royals, thick and heavy, complete with the blakey metal quarter tip across the bottom of the heel? Or smooths, same as the brogues but without any brogue? Another popular shoe was the fringe-and-buckle loafer that looked a bit like a slip-on golf shoe. But the favourite for everyday use was the good old tried-and-tested Dr Martens. The boots or the shoe version were good for anything – you could play football in them (no need for expensive trainers), watch football in them, dance in them, wear them to school, climb in them, and, like some of the trendy young teachers at my school, teach in them. Above all, they were very comfortable. Monkey boots had been fashionable for a while. They came in a brown-turd colour with a hard, tractor-like sole. We thought of them as a bit of a down-market Doc Marten. As a youngster I'd once owned a pair but they were now buried deep in my wardrobe, well hidden from a possible dawn raid by the fashion police.

The final part of the great dressing-up ritual was the correct placing of your bluebeat hat – or pork-pie hat as some people liked to call them – a sort of narrow-brimmed trilby felt hat. They came in either dark-blue or black and you had to get the position of it just right on your head. Slightly to the right? Down over the eyes? No, far too naff. Right on the back of the head was how it should be worn. If in doubt, we'd just copy the West Indian boys, who carried them off with more style then we ever did. We bought our hats in a shop just off Brixton market where all the black and white skinheads mixed happily.

The truth was, we were in awe of them because they had real style as skinheads. Some of the things they wore looked so much better on them. They moved better on and off the dance floor. In some respects we tried to copy them in those early days.

We even adopted their music as our own. The sounds of the day were ska, bluebeat, reggae and Motown. If you owned a copy of *Tighten Up Volume Two*, you were nearly complete. It would be even better if you were spotted by your mates or some girls with it under your arm, having just bought it at your local record store. A couple of times a week we would go to a mate's house and crowd round a little portable record-player and dance to the latest sounds on the Trojan label. You could just about hear the music above the hissing and crackling coming from the mono player. Most of the records would be badly scratched and covered in greasy fingerprints and the needle on the arm of the player often had a big ball of fluff hanging from it. We'd dance to tunes like 'Long Shot Kick the Bucket', Desmond Dekker's 'The Israelites' and 'The Liquidator' by Harry J and His All-Stars.

There was no hint of embarrassment as we practised the new steps we'd seen the older boys doing at the Croydon Suite the week before. The session would be even better if there were a few girls dancing with us – especially if there were no parents about and we had the house to ourselves. After a bit of showing off and trying to catch the girls' eyes, we'd try to pair off with a bird and get them upstairs. No chance. They obviously didn't appreciate a bit of good dancing.

These deadly serious dance sessions also took place at the nearby youth club, which was run by a church mission. All the local girls and boys between the ages of eleven and sixteen would meet up at the club once a week. The doors opened at seven but normally there'd be a line of kids waiting outside by half past six. The helpers at the club would organise five-a-side football, table-tennis, darts and billiards in an effort to keep us off the streets. In a little kitchen off the main hall you could buy cups of tea, cold drinks, hot buttered toast, crisps and sweets. Contact with the opposite sex was strictly forbidden. Snogging was quickly broken up and frowned upon and treated as seriously as a mass brawl would have been.

Half an hour before we were sent home, the church helpers would round everyone up and usher them into a darkened side room. A few of the boys, me included, would try to make our escape, but the front doors would be covered by Skipper, the head of the club. Our next escape route was the men's toilet window, but it was usually locked and bolted. In the end we'd give in and sit in front of the film projector and the makeshift screen to be subjected to various short films about the Bible and other religious shit. I suppose it wasn't a bad deal. They supplied us with an evening's leisure in return for us sitting in the dark and pretending to watch Daniel in the lion's den. Most of us wouldn't be taking a blind bit of notice of how Daniel was getting on in his fight for survival and would be more interested in shoving our hands up a bird's kilt. Others would be lighting up a crafty fag. Colin probably couldn't wait to get home and have a wank – no doubt he'd seen the tops of a girl's legs as she'd sat down opposite him.

Every week without fail I'd ask if we could watch a blue film and every week Skipper would give me the same answer, and shake his head and smile. 'Martin, I think you could be a lost cause.'

Jesus will find you. That was the message that ended every night and was plastered all over the club walls. How many of our lot were found by Jesus I don't know. If I was Jesus, I don't think I'd have searched too hard among my mates.

One Saturday morning when Chelsea were away up north I was asked by the mission to turn out for their football team. It was made up not of kids from the club but of staff and helpers and church friends. A sort of 'wannabe vicar, save our souls' side. I said I would. The team we were playing against were from a rough council estate in New Addington. We made our way there in a fleet of cars and passed through the concrete jungle better known as Croydon. The playing-fields were a vast open space surrounded by red-brick houses that all looked the same. The pitch was a quagmire, a sea of mud. You could tell we were in a classy area by the Ford Cortina dumped behind the goalposts. Jacked up – the wheels were missing – and burnt out, it was nevertheless being put to good use by the local kids. They were using it as a grandstand from which to watch the match.

We got changed by the side of the pitch, as the dressing-rooms belonging to the estate had unfortunately been torched by some locals after their team's defeat in a cup game a few weeks earlier. One of their team made sure we were within earshot before saying how the police believed the visiting football team were the intended target of the arsonists.

The two sides took to the field and the referee brought the captains together. He gave it the usual old spiel about how he was in charge and that he wouldn't stand for any backchat and bad language. Our opponents' captain turned to his team and shouted, 'Let's get into these cunts and show 'em what we're made of!'

The ref could hardly blow his whistle for laughing, but he did manage a little peep, followed by a wave of his arms to show that the game had kicked off.

The very first tackle left one of our players semi-conscious in the mud, and after that the Good Lord's Rovers didn't seem to fancy the game. We soon found ourselves 4–0 down, and all our boys were interested in was keeping their kits clean. Another crunching tackle went in and I complained to the ref. 'Come on, ref, have a word about some of these tackles.'

'It's a man's game,' he said and waved away my protests.

'Well, if you were any sort of man, you'd stand up to these arseholes.'

The whistle blew for half-time and we found ourselves losing 8–0. One of the players' girlfriends went around and handed out some slices of orange. Our captain sucked on his orange and tried to rally his troops: 'Come on, chaps, we're still in with a shout. Let's not allow ourselves to be bullied out of the game. With the help of Jesus, we can still turn the whole thing around.'

'Well, let's hope Jesus can play centre-forward and he's brought his boots with him,' I said.

If looks could kill . . . Still, straight from the kick-off I got the ball in the centre circle, saw their keeper talking to someone standing behind his goal and obviously not paying attention. So I lobbed the ball over everyone's heads and into the back of the net. 'Yes, yes, yes! Take that, you great big fucking lard arse,' I shouted as I jumped up and down in front of their big centre-half. His hairy beard parted and I could see his teeth were gritted as he snarled at me.

'Fuck off, you little bit of shit before I break your fucking scrawny little neck!' said their captain.

'Shut yer mouth, fatso, and go on a diet,' I replied.

From then on I was a marked man. Tackles were flying in on me every time I touched the ball. Eventually they got me. I was out on the wing heading for their goal when a waist-high tackle took me down. As soon as I hit the deck another of their players came in from the side and, with studs showing, clattered me on the knee. The studs ripped into my flesh and my knee felt like it was exploding. Blood poured from the three-inch gash. I was in agony as I lay doubled up on the grass, holding my leg.

'That'll teach you to be so gobby, you silly little prick!'

A few of their players bent over me but I didn't reply. The stuffing had been knocked right out of me.

The game finished with us losing 16–1. We didn't bother to get changed but just jumped straight into the cars and tried to get out of there as quickly as we could.

As we pulled away, one of their players stood in front of the car, blocking our exit. 'Will you lads be coming back to our club house for a drink?' he asked with just a hint of sarcasm.

I wound down the window. 'No, I don't think so, mate. You see, we're just on our way there to burn it down.'

And we took off out of there.

Derby County was the next away game I figured I could raise enough money to get to. After the adventure at the Hawthorns every penny I earned was put away. There was a buzz going round the school that a few of the kids fancied going to this game, and those who were up for it had already started making the necessary arrangements over a fag at the back of the school playing-fields. It is said the battle of Waterloo was won on the playing-fields of Eton; perhaps the battle of Derby County would be won on the playing-fields of Pollards Hill High.

'They're no pushover,' warned Steve Williams, a Spurs fan from around our way. 'We went in their end and it went off all the way through the game. Even outside, we couldn't run them. They're one of the hardest teams up north. About a hundred of our lot went looking for them after the game and it wasn't long before we found them – or should I say they found us. They poured out of a side street and steamed into us. We did well for a while but then their sheer numbers just overpowered us and they ended up running us back to the station.'

Steve was no bullshitter, and he was one of the few local lads that actually did go to Tottenham. When he wandered off I noticed a few faces already didn't fancy a trip to Derby. So I tried to rally the troops.

'Yeah, but we're Chelsea. We're not the yids. Let's not forget it's us who takes the Park Lane every year.'

Everyone nodded solemnly. For most of them the Park Lane was the space on the Monopoly board next to Mayfair.

As the bell sounded for the end of the break we strolled back to our various classrooms.

There we were, a bunch of fourteen- and fifteen-year-olds, planning on travelling over a hundred miles north to watch a football match and have a punch-up with a load of strangers just because they supported their local team. And we would be in their town supporting our favourite football team. We saw nothing wrong or peculiar in this. Perhaps if schools were to teach things to do with the real world, maybe do more subjects such as social studies and teach things that children can look back at once they've left school so they would already know the answer to a problem that is cropping up, we'd be better served. If schools taught us how to fix a car and why it's not the done thing to steal a car, what drugs do and don't do, why it's wrong and the damage you can do if you hit someone over the head and steal their money, and how not to get girls pregnant, maybe Jesus would have found me and I'd be selling *War Cry* and playing not with girls but in the Salvation Army brass band.

Tooting Broadway underground station at nine o'clock on a Saturday morning. Only four of us bothered to turn up despite all the bravado and the earnest preparations on the school playing-field: me, Jeff, Tony and Midget Hayman. Midget's real name was Malcolm, but his four-foot frame and ginger hair earned him his nickname. Unbelievably, he had played in goal for the school team, but as expected was very poor in the air. He didn't seem to be very good when dealing with high crosses but coped with ground shots superbly, perhaps because he didn't have very far to dive. I didn't think he'd been to a Chelsea away game before, something it was rapidly becoming compulsory for any aspiring skin to have on his CV.

I felt a bit stupid for thinking that those other prats would show up. 'Should have known those wankers would bottle it,' I moaned. 'Anyone know what's happened to them?'

'Saw Mick and his two brothers last night,' said Tony. 'They said something about their nan's golden wedding party.'

'Yeah, and I bumped into Dave and Colin in the chippy last night, down by the fair green, and they said they'd both promised Colin's dad they'd help him dig his allotment. I don't believe one word of it, though,' said Jeff.

'And don't forget Peter's doing your milk round.'

'I give up,' I sighed.

We caught the tube to Euston only to discover that the train we needed to get to Derby was actually leaving from St Pancras, a ten-minute hike up the road. Inside Euston on the concourse were hundreds of football fans decked out in blue-and-white scarves, rosettes and bobble hats. Even with my lack of experience I could tell these were not Chelsea fans. We were all dressed nearly identically in our crombies with our woollen scarves tucked neatly inside our collars. We all wore white Levi's Sta-prest and oxblood high-leg Dr Martens polished to a high shine. This other crowd milling about wore ill-fitting suits or jeans that sagged around the arse. Some wore anoraks and duffle-coats and grubby, flasher-like macs. A few of the older ones carried thermos flasks and rolled-up newspapers.

Without realising what was happening, a small group had surrounded us. 'Werr yew lads goin', den?' asked one of them. There was no mistaking that accent. John Lennon with a runny nose was addressing us. They were scousers without a doubt, and the blue and white told us they were Everton.

'Derby,' answered Jeff, staring straight into his eyes.

They looked us up and down. We all knew about the trend for rival fans to pinch one another's scarves, but this bunch seemed interested in everything we were wearing. One of them stood in front of me and ran his fingers down the arm of my coat. He took a step forward and his forehead touched mine. 'Nice coat,' he said. 'You know, we can't get these in Liverpool.'

No fucking way, I thought. I'll swallow the scarf – Auntie Ida can always knit me another one – but if I go home without the crombie the old man will never let me live it down. And Mum? The thought frightened me more than any scouser on this concourse. Life wouldn't be worth living – and not just for me but the scouser foolish enough to pinch it. She'd drag me up to Merseyside and we'd go from door to door until we found the thief.

'Bus!'

Tony had spotted it, and sprinted off, the rest of us quickly following. So did the Evertonians. My mates jumped onto the platform at the back just as the bus began to pull away. A punch whistled past my ear as the others urged me to run faster. Now I knew how Lennon and McCartney must have felt with all those screaming girls chasing after them.

'Run! Run!' urged the others but the look on their faces told me they didn't think I was going to make it. A scouser tried to trip me up but all he succeeded in doing was sending himself sprawling across the pavement. My chest felt like it was about to explode. I drew level with the back of the bus and jumped on as my mates grabbed hold of me, but the scarf around my neck was getting tighter as the cast of *A Hard Day's Night* clung on to me. The bus gathered pace and they were forced to let go, landing in a heap in the road. We shouted and jeered at them as if it were they who were running from us.

We jumped off the bus at St Pancras without paying and swaggered into the station on a bit of a high. We'd kept our clobber and come out of it in one piece. Chelsea fans were everywhere, standing around in small groups, chatting excitedly.

'I'd love to see them scumbag northern wankers try it on now,' I said to the others. 'Can you imagine that scouse bastard going up to Eccles? "Excuse me, mate, would you mind handing over that suede jacket you've got on. You see, we can't get them in Liverpool!" His feet wouldn't touch the fucking ground. He'd be lying flat out in seconds!' We all laughed at the thought.

The train was due to leave at 11.30 and the departure board indicated it was a 'football special'. This would be my first time on one of these fabled trains. They should have been called 'football not-very-specials' because they were dire. Competition for seats was intense and us younger lads normally had to travel for two or three hours standing or sitting on the floor of the aisle. If you were dead lucky, you could perch yourself on the arm of an older boy's seat. The heating was never turned on and the lights rarely worked. There were no refreshments sold on board though most people got round this by stocking up with crisps, Mars Bars, cans of Pale Ale and Watney's Red Barrel. On this train, one generous bloke was passing round a big red can of Party Seven bitter, which he'd opened with a Swiss army knife. I sat there and prayed it wouldn't get to me, but it did. It weighed a ton as I lifted it to my mouth. There was no way I was going to swallow the contents of this germ-infested can. I pretended to take a large gulp but the smell of fag smoke and bad breath nearly made me puke. I let out a loud burp and wiped my mouth with the back of my hand. 'That was fucking handsome.'

Everyone seemed to be unwrapping fresh packets of Park Drive, Embassy or No. 6. Midget pulled out a quarter-pound bag of rhubarb-and-custard boiled sweets and started passing them round. We were embarrassed to accept them among adult company but a sweet is a sweet. My biggest fear was he'd whip out *The Beano* or *The Dandy* from inside his crombie.

We sucked on our sweets and listened to the talk going on around us. Some of the older lads had been up to Derby before and kept warning us that their crew were no mugs. 'Crew' seemed to be the term for a gang of supporters. For me it conjured up images of nautical men in striped shirts with beards and big gold earrings, covered in tattoos and singing sea shanties. 'Crew' soon became a dated term and no firm or mob has been described as such for many years now. It was the same as fans from the lower leagues calling themselves a 'barmy army' – I mean, how fucking naff could you get?

One bloke who fancied himself as a bit of a leader for the day but who was little older than me, stood up on a seat and addressed the carriage: 'When we arrive at Derby we must all stick together.'

Fairly obvious, I thought. We all nodded.

'When we come out of the station we must keep it tight and walk along the road together.'

Again we all nodded.

'Then we all go in their end of the ground. Together.'

We all looked at each other, open-mouthed.

'Fucking hell! It looks like we're going in their end!' laughed Tony nervously.

Suddenly Midget jumped to his feet. 'Men, could I have your attention for a few minutes. I'd just like to endorse what that young man was saying about Derby being a dangerous place for visiting football fans. A Spurs friend of mine from school was saying how –'

But before he could finish Jeff had stuck his hand over his mouth and dragged him down on the floor. 'What the fuck are you playing at? We're on a train full of Chelsea, and you're talking about your *Spurs* mates.'

Midget got to his feet and brushed himself down. He had tears in his eyes and I almost felt sorry for him as he mumbled, 'Sorry. I'm sorry. I didn't mean it.'

To be honest, I was more embarrassed that he'd mentioned school than I was about him admitting knowing a Tottenham fan.

Finally the train began to slow down and it looked like we were approaching Derby station. Heads popped out the windows up and down the entire train.

'We're here!'

Doors flew open and eight hundred fans jumped off the still moving train.

'*Chelsea! Chelsea! Chelsea!*' boomed out and echoed all over the station. It was so loud at one point that I thought the roof was going to lift off. Passengers waiting on the other platforms gathered up their belongings and hurried off. Mothers pulled their kids towards them and the station staff locked themselves away in their wooden cabins. We joined the river of fans flowing out of the station and pushed as fast as we could to the front. We had this idea in our heads that the top boys couldn't manage without us and that they would struggle without our back-up.

The usual suspects were marching together at the front. Eccles glanced back over his shoulder at the human snake winding its way up the road behind him and he smiled proudly. Greenaway made notes in a little pocketbook as he walked along. Maybe he would one day turn all his adventures into a book. Premo, the Webbs and Jesus kept the front line nice and tight. These guys were the Shed superstars, and here I was rubbing shoulders with them.

The streets and houses were so different to what you saw around south London. West Bromwich had been a wasteground but here was row upon row of terraced houses – and none of them had front gardens. I'd love to have a paper round here, I thought to myself. I wonder if you'd get the same money, or if the newsagent would just give you more houses to deliver to.

I also noticed that not many houses had net curtains up at the front windows whereas at home everyone had nets hanging up to stop people like my mum peering in to their front rooms. We walked past a window and we could see an old man sitting at his dining-room table, tucking into a roast dinner. He was so close that if the window had been open I could have leant in and pinched a spud off his plate.

What did these Derby residents make of us? We were a strange army with our long dark overcoats and shaven heads. They didn't look scared – after all, strange-looking people from far away places visited Derby every other Saturday – but they did look a bit bewildered. I don't think football supporters from other parts of the country were so dominated by skinheads, the way the teams from London were at the time.

At a crossroads two policemen on horseback, the first we had seen, guided us straight on. To our left we got our first glimpse of Derby fans dressed in their dark-blue-and-white scarves. They kept their distance. As we drew level with a pub the crowd drinking outside in the sunshine shuffled in and bolted the door. Through the windows we could see them standing on tables and chairs, craning their necks to get a better view of this London invasion.

A fish-and-chip shop was up ahead, and a good few of the lads made a beeline for the door. This was one of the great mysteries of the world, football supporters and their quest for junk-food. I've seen some blokes risk life and limb for a pie and chips. I've seen people nicked in pursuit of a battered sausage. Why? The longest special journeys were three to four hours. We'd go that long at home without eating and, anyway, most of us would have been filling our faces with chocolate. So why the love affair with greasy chip shops? The Derby constabulary were having none of it, anyway, and began forcibly removing any Chelsea fans that had joined the queue.

The ground loomed up ahead and we kept quiet behind Eccles

and his merry men. They knew where they were going, all right, and so did the hundreds tagging along behind.

The mob came to a halt outside a row of turnstiles and for a moment it looked like the planned assault on the Derby end was going to be aborted. Then, without a word being said, the crowd pushed through the entrance. In the mayhem, we were lifted and carried along without our little legs touching the ground. Once inside we were all surprised to find that we were not standing behind the goal, but on the side facing the players' tunnel. It had never occurred to me that an end could be anywhere other than behind the goal. The police had not tried to stop us coming in and the rest of the Chelsea mob were still streaming in behind us.

'This is their end, all right,' I heard this massive skinhead say to his mate. 'Derby always come in late,' he went on, looking across to the entrance.

' Be ready for them. Don't forget they've held this end against both Arsenal and Spurs this season.'

Derby County had come from nowhere to being one of the best sides in the country, so it was only right their boys had to get some sort of respectable mob together. Brian Clough had come along and was like a breath of fresh air for Derby. His face was forever popping up on our TV screens. My dad, for one, loved him, and when he was on *Match of the Day* the programme would become interesting. He was a very charismatic character who actually said what he thought, and he didn't trot out the same old clichés like some managers did. He spoke from the heart and was one of the very few managers who were brave enough to do that. (Years later he provided one of my most treasured televised football moments when, as the manager of Nottingham Forest, he came on to the pitch and clipped the ear of some kid who had dared to run on to the field of play.)

The Chelsea players came out on to the pitch in their best John Collier suits for a pre-match turf inspection and I got talking to my mate John from Paddington.

'You ain't gonna believe what happened to me,' he said. 'I dived into the fish-and-chip shop up the road when this copper walks in and shouts for all Chelsea supporters to get out and carry on up to the ground. A couple leave but because I'm at the front of the queue I keep me nut down and order pie and chips. Anyway, the copper must have heard me ordering because he comes up behind me and grabs me by the ear and slings me out of the shop. "You going to the Baseball Ground," he shouts. Passers-by stop and stare. "No," I say, "I'm going to the football – I don't like baseball!" and with that he boots me right up the arse and tells me to fuck off to the ground with the rest of the animals, and if he sets eyes on me again I'd be spending the night in the cells. No one told me Derby's ground is called the Baseball Ground! Why the fuck did they name the ground after another sport?'

We all had a good laugh at this. John was genuinely put out.

The teams ran out on to the pitch and the whole end roared their support. Suddenly the people in front were being pushed back into us. Kids were trying to stay upright while others tried to reverse themselves under the crush barriers.

'You never take the pop side! You never take the pop side!'

No one knew what was happening but this chant was going up over and over again down below from where we are standing.

'What the fuck is the pop side?' I asked Jeff, who just shrugged his shoulders and stood on his tiptoes to try and see what was going on at the bottom of the terrace.

The whole crowd was being pushed sideways and a row of coppers positioned themselves in the middle of the terrace. Now it was the Chelsea hordes' turn to push sideways and forwards. In front of us appeared a three-foot-high metal fence. The line of Old Bill tried to stop anyone from climbing over it but they'd no chance as wave upon wave of the Chelsea mob found themselves in the Derby section. The Derby fans started to back off. They had stopped singing about us taking the pop side. A stand-off was on, but not for long as someone from our side decided to make a name for himself and steamed straight into the Derby fans who backed off even further. We followed and quickly filled up the spaces on the terraces. The coppers allowed us to stay in our newly conquered land and threw a protective ring around the Derby fans. We had great delight in reminding the Derby fans of the song they'd been singing five minutes earlier.

'*We've taken the fucking pop side! We've taken the fucking pop side!*' rang out from our ranks. And the day had been won. The Derby mob stood behind the line of coppers in complete silence. This was a textbook taking of an end, of the Eccles get-in-there-early mode favoured in the early 1970s. It was very effective (possession being nine-tenths of the law and all that) and most of the time the casualties were light on both sides. West Ham practised this to perfection at Chelsea for many years. I even recall them taking over the Shed by one o'clock and there was absolutely nothing we could do.

Just to make it difficult for themselves, at the end of the game, the police let both sets of fans leave the ground at the same time. The Derby fans seemed to volunteer to head off in one direction, as the police gave us an escort of sorts through the narrow terraced streets. A policeman with a megaphone that looked like it had come free with that week's *Buster* comic walked alongside us, issuing instructions. This time the good citizens of Derby stood on their doorsteps to watch as we passed just feet from their doors. This strange army of young shaven-headed youths was once again on the move. One man, dressed in a fetching string vest, didn't seem to trust us and stood on his doorstep stroking a huge Alsatian. The smirk on his face said it all.

A few kids pressed their noses up against the window of one of the houses and peered inside to see if they could catch the football results. A little black-and-white telly was flickering away in the corner. 'The Yids lost!'

Up went a big cheer.

'Fulham won!'

Another big cheer.

The sound of shattering glass prompted the locals to retreat into their houses. The front doors slammed and the curtains were drawn. A Derby mob about two hundred-strong had appeared from a side street and they launched a barrage of bottles and bricks at our throng. When the ammo dried up they stopped dead in their tracks and didn't steam into us. They left a safety buffer of about twenty feet. We took the initiative and ran into them. This time they stood and fought toe to toe for a few seconds. But before anything serious could happen, mounted police galloped into the fray and scattered the main combatants.

The Derby boys moved off and regrouped further up the road, no doubt happier they'd made a better show than inside the ground.

The railway station was in front of us now and the policeman with the megaphone was telling us our train was waiting and that we should hurry and get on our way. A group of about fifty older Chelsea lads ignored the copper and walked straight past the station, ducking right at the first turning. We followed. A dozen Derby boys stood in the middle of the road and waved us towards them.

A man of about twenty took control. 'Walk, don't run,' he ordered. 'There will be more of these northern wankers hiding round the corner.'

For the first time I was a bit worried. This was a quiet side street and there were no police about. It was just them and us. And what about my clobber? The old girl would murder me if I ripped or lost anything.

Then the Derby boys broke into a sprint and came at us, and they just kept flowing from around the corner. Twelve soon became fifty. A Derby boy in a duffle-coat aimed a kick at me. A duffle-coat, for fuck's sake! It even had the wooden toggles. I bet his mum dressed him this morning. I caught him nicely on the hooter, and he backed off with his mates. But the big fellas at the front were still fighting with one another. The sight of some of their numbers running unsettled them, and soon most of them were back-pedalling. One or two of their boys had been knocked to the ground. The last few disappeared for good as the Old Bill rounded us up and shepherded us back to the station.

One of the bigger Chelsea lads came up and patted me and Midget on the head. 'You done well there, you two. What's your names?'

We told him and our little chests puffed right out. How bad was that? A mention in dispatches on only our second tour of duty. We forgot to tell him that while it had all been going off we were shitting ourselves.

On the train journey home we were allowed to sit in the same compartment as the main faces. We listened to all the post-battle analysis. The day was judged as a huge success. We had succeeded where Tottenham and Arsenal had failed and we had given a good all-round account of ourselves. To be privy to all this was like a dream come true. When we got off the train at St Pancras, the older boys who were sitting with Eccles and company said goodbye and called me and Midget by our names. I know that as a kid you're meant to get a kick out of passing your eleven-plus or winning a cross-country cup for the school, but for me this recognition was the biggest thrill of my life so far. The buzz was unbelievable.

During the bus journey from Tooting to Mitcham, Jeff and I chatted about how the boys at school would never believe the day's events. Jeff was gutted that Midget and I had been with our top boys in the row at the back of the station. 'Trust me and Tony to lose you, and then it goes right off.'

Tony and Midget headed off towards their houses and Jeff and I strolled home down Gas Works Alley. Jeff pulled a hanky from his coat pocket. Wrapped inside was a battered cold steak-and-kidney pie. Bits of fluff and pocket fur and other questionable substances seemed to have become attached to it, but Jeff was unperturbed and ripped a chunk out with his teeth. 'Emergency supplies,' he tried to say as bits of pastry flew from his lips. 'Sorry, Kingy, but I had to wait until the other two had fucked off so that I didn't have to share it four ways. I got it in that chip shop at Derby. D'you want a bite?'

Now that's what I call a real mate!

THREE

Fair Dos

Monday morning and it was back to school. At break, up at the tennis courts, I conducted my own enquiry into the non-appearance of the apparently enthusiastic Chelsea Shed boys.

'When we left school on Friday afternoon we were meant to be taking a massive mob up north,' I sneered. 'Pollards Hill was supposed to be well represented.'

The catalogue of feeble excuses was trotted out only to be met with hoots of 'Shitters!' from Midget, Tony and me.

A crowd gathered as we launched into the tale of our day-trip to the Midlands. 'You should have seen Martin crack this northern geezer. He was a great big lump in a donkey jacket – must have been twenty-five at least,' said Midget. (Seventeen, possibly, and it was a duffle-coat, but never let the truth get in the way of a good story.)

'We stood our ground and we ran them after the game,' I summed up.

'Yeah, but *we* smashed up our special on the way home, and then got off in the countryside and took over a town.' This from Ruben, a Spurs fan who was claiming he'd been involved in a notorious incident a few weeks previously, when five hundred Yids smashed up the special taking them back to London. The train had been halted and its human cargo thrown out into the wilds of the English countryside. The Spurs mob terrorised the rural community, smashing windows and causing damage to property. Some locals returned to their homes that night to find they had been burgled and their places vandalised. The police spent hours rounding up the Spurs fans but rumour had it that calm was only restored after the police threatened to call in the Chelsea Shed boys. The incident made the national news.

'Big fucking deal,' I interjected, 'any prick can smash up a train. Trains don't hit back but Derby fans do.'

Ruben rubbed his hands together nervously and curled his lip as if to snarl out a reply. He knew what I'd said was the truth, but the tension was broken when a football was kicked into our midst and without further ado we split into two teams for a twenty-a-side game. All talk of aggro soon subsided as we reverted to the more familiar fantasies of being our favourite footballer. I was Charlie Cooke that day, while Tony announced he was Peter Osgood and Midget was Alan Hudson.

'Cooke has the ball, he beats one, he goes past another, he rounds the keeper . . . surely he must score! The crowd go wild as he passes to Osgood!'

Tony took over the ball and the commentary: 'Sooooperb effort!' he gasped as his shot sailed hopelessly over everyone's head and bounced out of sight onto the canteen roof.

Every day we'd take the 118 bus from Pollards Hill to Mitcham Fairgreen home from school, passing the local grammar school en route. Every one of us climbed on the seats of the top deck and hurled abuse out of the windows at these posh kids neatly attired in their striped blazers, caps and flannels.

'Hello, Walter! Hello, Cedric!' we jeered. 'Can Cuthbert come around for a spot of tea?'

They sensibly ignored the taunts. It wasn't their fault they had the audacity to pass their eleven-plus exam. But this was how it was. We're not even talking about a public school here; an institution like Eton was beyond our comprehension. Many of these so-called toffee-nosed kids would have come from the same background as us, but maybe their parents showed a bit more interest in their children's education – or the kids themselves were slightly better honed, with the ability to remember pointless dates.

The victimisation and prejudice wasn't just one-sided, though, and besides, we were conditioned to think and behave this way. For instance, the undoubted stars of *The Beano* were the Bash Street Kids, and with a readership of a few million there were not many English schoolchildren who were not exposed to them for some years. Danny, Plug, Smiffy, Fatty and friends often decamped down to the local grammar school to let loose with their catapults and water-pistols on the despised 'swots'. In the same comic Dennis the Menace spent many happy hours bullying Walter, the smart brylcreemed boy with a love of homework. So the stereotypes were reinforced; we were the football-loving cheeky cockneys who scoffed pie and mash and fish and chips, and they were Lord Snooty and chums who loved playing rugger, fox-hunting, sailing and polo, and who were just biding their time until we would be their chauffeurs or the gardeners on their large country estates.

Every evening after school my friends and I would arrange to meet somewhere. One evening we all decided to go to the fair which had set up on Mitcham Common for a week. The fair was a big event in the social calendar. It was very exciting to a young kid, with all the rides, the sweets, the hustle and the bustle and the tacky prizes, the coconuts and the candyfloss. But now that we were teenagers, it was an arena for showing off your new clothes, meeting and hopefully shagging new crumpet from out of town, and posing and posturing with other gangs.

The two big nights for the fair were Friday and Saturday. As dusk fell, families and younger children would drift off home, clutching the goldfish won on the hoop-la. As the evening went on, youths from all parts of south London descended on the fair. The dodgem cars was the main meeting place and anyone who was anyone could be spotted draped around the perimeter of the large circular platform that served as the racetrack. Here was a right melting-pot of youth culture. Skinheads predominated and you'd see big ones and little ones, old ones and young ones, black ones and white ones. Close by stood some greasers or rockers, with their lank black hair and oil-stained sleeveless jean jackets. The fairground seemed to be the last bastion of this particular breed. Six or seven years earlier they had been terrorising England while waging war with the Mods on the beaches of the southern coastal resorts, but now their numbers had dwindled, perhaps because they were unable to change – unlike their arch-enemies, the Mods, who had found it easier to progress with fashion and become skinheads. Even a few of their older cousins, the Teddy Boys, were present in their drapes, slicked-backed hair and winklepicker shoes. Strangely, we didn't regard the Teds as dinosaurs. As outlandish as their clobber was to us, they still had our utmost respect, even if they didn't strike fear into us.

The music on this ride, barely audible over the whirring and crashing of the bumper cars, was all rock'n'roll and early '60s stuff. There was Elvis singing about keeping his blue suede shoes clean, and someone else telling Laura he loved her. This type of music told me who the fairground people believed their customers were.

As well as this parade of youth culture 1955–70 we saw the fairground workers themselves. You couldn't help admiring them and not be a touch jealous at the way they glided between the fast-moving cars and attached themselves to the poles that joined the car to the sparking wire roof. Then, leaning forward in the car, they would allow a couple of skinhead girls to pop a two-bob piece into the palm of their grubby outstretched hand. The girls' fingers often lingered a shade longer than a normal cash transaction should take. Then the guys would go into show-off mode and dance and skip across the metal surface, deftly swerving to avoid oncoming cars and instinctively knowing which cars had paid and which hadn't.

These boys weren't bothered about the current fashions. They were hillbilly types and had more in common with the greasers than with us. But there was just a touch of romance in their lifestyle which lifted them beyond those everyday allegiances. It's strange to think now when youths aspire to be commodity traders in the City or pinstriped entrepreneurs, we could imagine nothing better than to travel with the fair.

On reflection, the root of all this envy was their perceived pick of the women. While there was no doubt that the local girls were like putty in their hands, the reality was, to my mind, that this was all fantasy, because, unlike Butlins for example, the fairground lacked the two essential ingredients that make the possibility of casual sex among young people a reality: alcohol and a place to do it.

When I got home after school I didn't bother to wash. Instead, I just splashed on my trusty Brut aftershave from the little green bottle with the chain and medallion hanging from its neck. I even went as far as dabbing a handful around my nuts because maybe – just maybe. That was my nightmare scenario – pulling a bird who's willing but when you whip out your cory she flees the country because of the smell of it. If I could smell my dick a mile off, it would certainly put a stop to my chances of getting into a young lady's knickers. Brut disguised a whole multitude of sins.

Besides my groin area, I'd use it under my arms and sometimes on my feet, which for some reason I couldn't understand had started to stink for England. Must've been those socks I'd had on for the last six months. The thing with socks was they never really got dirty, and even if they did, they were hidden away inside your boots or shoes, so who was going to see them? It was only the smell that warned you they might need changing.

Resplendent in my ice-blue Sta-prest and red braces, I was just about to dash out of the house and meet the others when I noticed a note left by the old girl. 'Gone to bingo,' it read, 'back at five thirty. Dad in from work the same time – put the potatoes, which are in a saucepan, on a low gas for your father's tea.'

Shit. I looked up at the clock. It was nearly half past five. The old girl's canister would explode if I hadn't done as she asked. Bang on the dot, I could hear the front door opening and the squeaking of Dad's bike as he wheeled it into the hall. I quickly lit the gas and shoved a lid on the pot and then sprinted through to the front room where I sprawled out on the settee and pretended I was watching *Blue Peter*.

'All right, boy? What's silly bollocks Noakes or whatever his name is up to now? Parachuting off the Leaning Tower of Pisa?' He rubbed his hands together. 'What's your mother made for tea, then?' Dad was talking more to himself than me. 'I just hope it ain't bleedin' sausages again. I'm beginning to think that's all your mother knows how to cook – sausage, mash and onions. D'ya know what, son, after nearly twenty-five years I've started to get a bit bored with the same grub every night. What d'ya reckon?'

I think he was only joking and was trying to invite me back into the conversation he was having with himself as he took off his coat and tweed cap and hung them up on the back of the door. He carried on rabbiting about being married to the same woman for over twenty years but to be honest I found myself more interested in what was happening on *Blue Peter*. Silly bollocks Noakes, as Dad called him, was canoeing down whitewater rapids, and Dad's voice seemed to fade away into the distance. But the old man talking about sausages certainly bought a smile to my face. We had a secret about sausages, me and Mum.

A few weeks before, she had asked me (or should I say *ordered* me) to cycle down to the butcher's at Mitcham Fairgreen and pick up some sausages. Trouble was, it was pissing down with rain and by the time I reached the shop I was wringing wet.

'Lovely day,' said the butcher as he handed me the wrapped-up bangers. I clasped the brown paper bag under my arm as I steered the bike back one-handed through the monsoon towards home. The strong wind was blowing the rain into my face and I kept telling myself there wasn't that much further to go. I didn't notice until I got off the bike that the rain had caused the bag to split and the sausages had fallen out and wrapped themselves around the spokes of the back wheel and mudguard. I handed the wet, torn, empty bag to Mum.

'You fucking dopey idiot. Where's the fucking –' and she looked down at the wheel and saw bits of sausage all mashed and soaking entwined in the spokes. 'You're fucking useless, I can't trust you to do anything. What'll I give your dad for his tea? He'll go fucking mental if there's no dinner on the table. Well, I'll let you tell him, you stupid little bastard.'

'What about me?' I appealed, 'I might get pneumonia or even flu!'

'Fuck you. Get them off that wheel now. I'll dip them in some flour and fry them, he won't know any different.'

She meant it, too, and that's what she did. She served it up for the old man's dinner with boiled potatoes and fried onions and he wolfed the whole lot down. Mum and me waited in the kitchen, giggling.

'That was handsome, love,' he shouted from the front room, as we heard him scraping the last forkful off the plate. 'I reckon you've been watching that Fanny Craddock again.'

She smiled at me and nodded as if to say I told you so, and walked into the front room. As she lifted the tray from Dad's lap he leant back into the armchair, and lit his pipe. 'What's for pudding, love?'

'Back light and a special inner-tube custard,' I said as I stood in the kitchen doorway, grinning.

'Tell me, love, what is that scatty bastard on about now?'

Mum aimed a kick towards my arse and I scampered out the door to meet up with the others.

When I arrived at the 64 bus-stop, the rest of the boys were already there, along with about forty other people waiting patiently in an orderly queue. The bus would take us to the Croydon end of Mitcham Common. We stood around chatting, leaning up against the newsagent's window. When the bus turned up we jumped straight on and up the stairs. Fuck all that waiting in a queue. We took a seat each, leaning back against the window and stretching our legs and boots across the entire seat. We all sat at the back. It wasn't cool to sit at the front, although it wasn't so long ago when the front seats were much prized and you'd grip the bar and pretend you were driving the bus.

There was lots of noise as we tried our best to get the rest of the passengers to take notice of us. A couple of the boys lit up fags and to add effect to the hard-man look they tilted their bluebeat hats over their eyes and dragged long and hard on the cigarette dangling from their lips, but being extra careful not to inhale any of the smoke. It would be so embarrassing suddenly to turn a funny shade of green in front of your mates and then throw your ring up. They say smoking can damage your health, but what they don't tell you is that it can also seriously damage your reputation among your friends. Almost all of us had on light-coloured Sta-prest trousers with the customary green grass stain on the knees. Each one of us, I was sure, felt we couldn't fail to pull dressed like this. We also felt the confidence that comes with being in a gang. There was lots of talk of us sticking together should anyone have a go at us.

'We'll be all right,' someone said. 'We know all the Pollards Hill lot.'

'And all the black boys from Croydon.'

An old lady, aged about thirty-five, came up the spiral staircase and looked hard at us draped all over the red-checked seats.

'Take your feet off the seat, please,' she said to Tony.

Tony didn't move. He looked at us and then he looked at the woman. 'Why?'

'Because someone has to sit there, like your mum or your nan, maybe, and they wouldn't like to sit on a seat covered in mud which has been left on the seat by some yobbo who thinks it's clever to sit with his feet up.'

There was no answer to that, and I could see the embarrassed look on his face as it went from red to a deep purple. If the woman had said one more thing I'm sure he would have burst into tears. He lifted his legs from the seat with a slow, exaggerated effort and let both feet fall to the floor.

Once we could see the lights of the big wheel towering above all the other constructions adorned with coloured lightbulbs we swung around the pole at the top of the bus, tumbled down the stairs like a herd of elephants and jumped off the moving bus. '*Yeeha!*' someone screamed, and for a split second we were nine again. Then we remembered and slowed right down, composed ourselves and strolled into the fair like the young hard nuts we aspired to be.

I loved the fair as a little kid. I remember being amazed after it packed up and left town how the grass had been literally worn away in just a week through people walking around. I knew all the rides so well: the dive-bomber that seemed as high as the Crystal Palace tower when you were up in it; the wall of death, a ride where the floor suddenly fell from under your feet and, as it whirled round at great speed, you were sucked up against the wall and couldn't move; the bumper cars, my favourite because it was one of the few rides that stayed on the ground; the Big Wheel and the newer rides, where you were flung around in little cars on the end of long, mechanised arms. If anyone asked me to go on a ride like that, I'd make the excuse that I'd not long had my tea. There was no way you'd catch me going on something like that. All my mates loved the so-called mad rides and thought it probably gave them a better chance with the girls. They'd go on something like the Waltzers and spin round at high speed, waving and shouting at the girls watching at the edge of the ride. I'd be standing on my own like a plum waiting for the boys to get off the rides. But if it was a straight choice between me heaving my guts up or staying on *terra firma*, my stomach would win over the chance to show off in front of a few schoolgirls. I'm sure a few of the others weren't that keen on getting slung around at 100mph but they didn't admit it.

I loved looking at the variety of human life on display. There were always huge men dressed in white string vests around. They had muscled arms like Popeye which were covered in tattoos and the misspelt names of former girlfriends. Some had 'Mum' and 'Dad' inked crudely on their knuckles and thick gold rope chains hanging from their bull-like necks. Women almost as huge would sometimes be tagging along behind them. I'd see elderly men with caps on, their skin brown and leathery, talking in what sounded like a foreign language, but the boys and I knew they were speaking Romany. I listened to it every day at home and at school, and to a lot of kids it was their mother tongue. Beautiful gypsy girls with long curly black hair fiddled with their gold hoop earrings. They walked around in groups but you wouldn't dare catch their eye. Suspicious-looking middle-aged men walked about alone, dressed in raincoats done up tightly with a big belt around the middle.

On one tent there was a sign which told us that for a sixpence we could go inside and see the Bearded Lady. Fucking bearded lady! I could see her any day of the week if I cared to go around Tony's nan's house!

The biggest crowd would gather outside the boxing booth where a man holding a microphone would introduce the spectators to a masked man and then throw down a challenge: 'If any local lad or man can last three two-minute rounds with the masked man, I will personally hand over £10.'

The crowd would fall silent and wait expectantly for someone brave or daft enough to enter the ring. The plan was that if the local hard-man or the village idiot wasn't available, another boxer who worked with the fair would act as a plant in the crowd. He would step forward and take up the challenge and the crowd would go wild.

'Ladies and gentlemen, we have found ourselves a brave challenger. What's your name, son?'

'Tommy Smith.'

'Tell me, son, have you ever boxed before?'

' No, sir, I haven't. But I feel kinda lucky tonight.'

What a liar! A nose as flat as a saddle bag across a horse's arse, his forehead covered in scar tissue, he can just about remember who he's meant to be, he's so punch drunk! And yet he's never boxed before? Let's hope he's a better boxer than he is an actor. The crowd rushed forward to pay the entrance fee. They had been whipped up into a mass frenzy and they wanted to see some blood after parting with their money. But there was only ever going to be one winner.

Tonight we nodded over at some black boys we knew and they nodded back. That was good. There was nothing worse than nodding at one of the top Mitcham or Croydon faces and they totally blank you, especially in front of your mates. Nothing better, though, than a known older face nodding or speaking to you first. A single 'All right, Martin?' from a top skin was enough to raise your credibility among your peers by several notches.

Next to the gate where they were loading up pairs of young lovers for the next Big Wheel ride was a punchball bag hanging from a machine with a dial which told you how hard your punch was. A few of the Pollards Hill gang were dropping coins in and punching away for the benefit of their girlfriends who stood back and watched. A black kid from Croydon soon showed everyone up. He strolled over to the machine, inserted his money, turned round and walked back two paces, and then let go a right hook so hard it sent the ball spinning round and round. The lights went out and the dial let out a humming noise, like it was in pain. He'd done this with hardly any effort. We looked in awe at this kid's power. Perhaps the expression 'punching someone's light out' comes from incidents like these. He was about seventeen and wore a loose-fitting basketball vest which allowed us to study (hopefully without him noticing) his impressive physique.

A few of the girls from school had gathered around. 'We've just been admiring his muscles,' said one.

'So fucking what?' I replied, my pride dented by their obvious admiration for this interloper. I didn't say it too loud, because although Leroy had strolled off he was still within earshot.

'He's from Croydon,' said one of the other girls authoritatively, as if she knew his every move. 'His two brothers are black belts in karate. We met them all at the Croydon Suite a couple of weeks ago. You should see them dance.'

'I can't wait,' I said sarcastically.

Fittingly, a hit of the time, 'Young, Gifted and Black', started to blast out from the dodgems' sound system, and us boys went into our well-rehearsed dance routine. It raised a giggle from the girls and perhaps won back a smidgeon of the admiration they had just bestowed on Leroy. That was until the great man himself reappeared and joined in our moves. He was different gear, spinning round on one heel with his arms folded. Flash bastard, I was thinking. If there's a God, make him fall over and twist his fucking ankle – no, on second thoughts, let's go the whole hog: make it his neck.

Unable to compete, we drifted off, leaving the girls giggling and sighing at the great man's acrobatics.

'Hold up,' I said. 'I'm just going for a piss behind that caravan.'

'I wouldn't if I was you,' said Tony.

'Why's that then, Tone, just in case there's a guard dog chained up underneath the trailer?' I joked.

'No, Leroy might whip his dick out at the same time and show us all up again.'

I relieved myself up against the polished chrome of someone's caravan. Peeping inside the window as I pissed I couldn't believe the luxury. Large silk cushions were propped up against the back of the most beautiful flowered suite. Crown Derby china stood in a polished walnut display cabinet, a thick white shag-pile carpet covered the floor and fine lace curtains hung from the windows. In the corner was a colour telly, the screen almost as big as the one down at the Tooting Granada. You didn't get rooms like this in people's houses in Mitcham. The only person I knew who had a colour telly was Kevin Reeves's old man, Lenny. We used to go round there when Lenny was out and watch *Match of the Day*. The only other time I'd watched one was in the window of Radio Rentals, along with crowds of other people waiting at the bus-stop, on my way home from football matches. One summer I even joined a crowd of about sixty people pressed up against a shop window watching Rod Laver in action at Wimbledon. 'Look at how green the grass looks,' said one excited adult standing behind me.

'Soppy bastard,' I thought. Anyone would think the real world around us was in black and white. Still, that's the power of television.

I could hear my mates talking to a girl so I zipped myself up fast and jumped back into the fray. She stood among them looking well tidy with her long spider-cut hair hanging down to her shoulders, false eyelashes and just a bit too much lipstick.

I moved in for the kill. 'All right, love? I'm Martin.'

'Hello, Martin,' she smiled sweetly.

I looked beyond her shoulder to see if she had any mates with her.

'Fuck off, Kingy,' said Nicky Potter, elbowing me in the ribs, 'I saw her first.'

'Fancy taking a walk, sweetheart?' I continued, ignoring Nicky.

'I don't care,' she replied, which meant 'yes' in girl-speak.

I lifted my elbow slightly and she slipped her hand through my arm.

Nicky's face began to change colour. His lip quivered and the veins in his neck were going purple. 'I said, Kingy, I saw her first, or are you fucking deaf?'

'Now, now, boys, don't fight over me,' said the girl.

Nicky stood in front of us, blocking our path. I wasn't going to give way, it was my forearm her delicate fingers were resting on. I didn't want to fight Nicky and I don't think he wanted to fight me, but I could see he was riled. So it was stalemate.

'Tell you what,' Tony suggested, 'why don't you ching up and whoever wins gets off with the girl?'

'Best of three?'

Nicky nodded. The girl's mouth dropped open in amazement as we gambled for her favour. The boys gathered round in a circle. Nicky and I stood eye to eye with our hands clasped behind our backs. I won the first game and Nicky won the second, so it all rested on the third. Tension mounted and we pushed in closer. What we thought we were playing for, I'm not sure. A bunk-up? A wank? A bit of tit? A snog? And what say had the prize in all this? None. No one had even been bothered to ask her name.

A cheer went up as Nicky won. The girl dutifully dropped my arm and walked over to the jubilant victor. I watched crestfallen as they squeezed through the gaps between the caravans that circled the fairground site and disappeared into the darkness of the woods beyond.

Jeff looked at me. Tony looked at Jeff. I looked at Tony.

'Shall we?'

No answer. It didn't need one. We followed into the darkness. We tiptoed behind them and watched them kissing as they fell to the ground. We dived behind a caravan, eventually crawling underneath it so we could watch from the same level. They were snogging away and Nicky, like his arm had nothing to do with the rest of him, was attempting to push his hand up inside her Fred Perry. She, also acting like her arm had nothing to do with what her lips were doing, was pushing it away. He stopped kissing and looked at her, almost begging: 'Oh, go on, just a bit of tit,' he moaned and we put our hands to our mouths to stifle the giggles.

'No,' came the stern reply.

Nicky entered the negotiating phase: 'How about if I just touch them on the outside of your top.'

'No.'

' What about a wank, then?' hissed Nicky not very seductively, nibbling her ear because perhaps he'd seen that work in a film.

'You disgusting pig!' she shouted as she jumped up and started brushing blades of grass and leaves from her clothes. 'Just what do you take me for, you fucking bastard!'

She spun around and marched back into the fair, passing just feet from where we were lying. We buried our heads in the grass.

'Come back! Come back! You've got it all wrong!' whined Nicky.

We waited till he'd gone and then crawled out from underneath the caravan, doubled up with laughter. The tears were streaming down our cheeks. We couldn't catch our breath, and we were laughing so much that my sides ached as we stepped back into the music and bright lights of the fair. We saw Nicky emerge back through the ring of caravans one or two vehicles further up and quickly adopted straight faces.

'How did you get on, Nick?' asked Tony

'Shagged the arse off it,' he boasted.

'What, you actually got her drawers off, then?' enquired Jeff.

'Course. I ain't going to shag it with her knickers still on, am I? Lovely body on it.'

'Big tits or little tits?' I asked.

'About average, but very firm, with long nipples.'

'Let's smell your fingers, then.'

'Fuck off, you perverts.'

'You gonna see her again, then, Nick?'

Nicky's confidence was rising by the second. To do the things he claimed to have done with the girl, he would have had to have been behind the caravan for two hours rather than the two minutes he was actually there. 'No,' he said. 'I told her right at the beginning I ain't looking for no serious relationship, just a quick shag, or maybe meet up once a month just to get my winkle wet.'

'And she was all right about that?' I asked. I wanted to build him up just a little bit more before puncturing his self-esteem.

'Looks like she does want to see you again,' observed Jeff, 'and by the looks of it she's got your future brother-in-law and his mates with her.'

'Maybe she's just found out she's pregnant,' I joked.

Steaming towards us was a boy of about eighteen, along with Nicky's fiancée and about a dozen other miscreants. The big one at the front had a donkey jacket on with a claret-and-blue scarf tucked inside the collar. Dried spit had gathered at the corner of his lips. He clenched his fists as he spoke. 'Right! Which one of you wankers has been upsetting my sister?' He stared at each of us in turn while his mates stood behind him, trying to look hard. 'Which one of you clowns has been trying to touch my sister's tits? Eh? Eh?'

'Thought you told us you shagged it,' whispered Tony out of the corner of his mouth.

Nicky's eyes were fixed to the floor. I don't know if it was through fear or embarrassment, but he wouldn't look up. There was a silence you could cut with a knife as both sides weighed up what to do next.

Jeff took the initiative. 'Who do you support?' he asked the girl's brother.

'What's that got to do with this?' retorted the older boy, surprised by this deflection.

'West Ham, are you? Or maybe Aston Villa fans on a day-trip to London to see your cockney relatives who live in the smoke? Perhaps you're Burnley fans. No, I reckon you're Hammers fans, probably season-ticket-holders and stand on the North Bank every week.'

Big brother sensed that Jeff wasn't exactly scared of him, and he and his mates began to fidget nervously. Smiles came to our faces and the nervous looks disappeared. Good old Jeff.

'We're Crystal Palace fans, actually,' volunteered one of their gang.

At that, Jeff brought up his fist from his waist and cracked big brother straight on the jaw. He went down on his knees, mumbled something about 'you've had it' and passed out. His gang, including sis, took flight.

'Why did you ask him if he was West Ham?' I asked Jeff as we dashed away leaving the boy in a crumpled heap on the deck.

'Well, if he was a West Ham fan, I might have thought twice about hitting him. You see, West Ham's mob are a bit tasty, and unlike Palace boys, they hit back. When I realised that they were Palace, well – he just had to go.'

The evening wore on and we'd had our bit of fun, and although none of us admitted it to each other we all had to be home by certain times – all before ten o clock – so we walked off the fair and ran across the road to jump onto a bus we saw approaching. As we scrambled aboard and the bus pulled away we could see a group of youths running towards us. It was the Palace lot and their number, it was clear, had been swollen by a few of the fairground workers with their lank greasy hair, dirty jeans and well-worn bumper boots. Scruffy bastards.

The bus gathered speed. We stood on the rear platform clinging to the pole and hurling insults at the motley crew pursuing us. Tony gave them the wankers sign and shouted, 'Come on, you Palace bastards, speed it up a bit, or don't you want to catch us?'

'Come on and have a go at the Chelsea Shed boys,' I hollered, cupping my hands around my mouth for extra volume as they began to lose ground on the fast-moving bus.

Then, to our horror, the bus pulled over to pick up some people who had flagged it down just outside the fair. The Palace mob now had a good chance of catching us and they began to loom closer. Now they were less than fifty yards away and closing. We were shitting it and praying the bus would pull away. *For fuck's sake, conductor, ring that fucking bell so that we can get away!* Twenty yards now and we could see the anger in their eyes and hear the abuse and what they're going to do to us. *Come on, driver, move this fucking bus!* We suddenly went very quiet and I for one was shitting bricks. Those fairground boys, all they do is fight, I thought, they probably carry blades – it saves on their knuckles and gets the aggro over quicker. One slash, swish or stab, a bit of blood and it's back to work. Easy. Why the fuck did Jeff hit that geezer? There really was no need. We could have talked our way out of it. Him sparking the geezer was funny at the time, but as payback time loomed, things were not looking good. The bell sounded and the bus rolled into life. We breathed a sigh of relief as at last we had a bit of distance between us and them. We hit fourth gear and a cloud of black smoke billowed from the exhaust pipe.

'You unfit Palace tossers!' we yelled.

More wanker signs were exchanged.

'See you down at Palace in a fortnight's time, you Chelsea wankers!' cried one of their boys nearest the bus. 'Bet you won't have the bottle to come into the Holmesdale end!'

But as the bus zoomed away into the night air, the Palace boys and their soap-dodging mates gave up the chase and we could see them heading back to the fair.

'Did you hear that prick?' I said to the others as we relaxed on the top deck, the panic over. 'Bet you won't come in the Holmesdale, he said, cheeky bastard. Who does he think we are, Watford or some-one?'

They had thrown down the gauntlet and we were determined to pick it up and walk into Selhurst Park, waving it around our heads.

Back at school the next day two things dominated the conversation: Nicky's love life and the forthcoming row at Crystal Palace. We told everyone at school about Nicky and his new-found love and what a charmer he was. For the rest of the week and nearly the rest of the term he got untold grief. The piss-taking was relentless and a whole batch of new nicknames sprang up. Boys and girls would shout, 'You cad, Potter!' after him down the corridor. He'd be walking through Mitcham and a car would drive past and out of the window someone would shout, 'Oi, Romeo, give us a bit of tit..Please. Just from the outside!' followed by howls of laughter. Poor old Nick, he had to put up with this for the rest of his schooldays.

Everyone I spoke to said they were up for the Palace game but I'd heard that before. So, just to make sure, I told everyone at the youth club, and then again on the Saturday at Stamford Bridge. I tried to stir up everyone standing in the Shed.

'Heard about Palace next week? Apparently they've challenged Chelsea to go in the Holmesdale end. Yeah, it's true, they reckon they're going to do Chelsea. I know, ridiculous, ain't it? Anyway, Eccles and Greenaway and the rest of the boys are well annoyed, so everyone's going.'

It worked a treat because by the time the second half got under way I'd heard my story back from at least half a dozen other people, and suitably exaggerated each time.

On the day of the game we met at one o'clock at Thornton Heath railway station which wasn't too far from our homes and only about a ten-minute trot to the ground. It was a cold, grey day, so most of us had our crombies on and our blue-and-white scarves tied tightly around our necks. Probably because it was much closer and cheaper than going to Derby, about thirty of our lot had turned up this time. As we got off the train at Thornton Heath we were met outside the station by fifty smiling faces from Pollards Hill. A few girls from school had tagged along as well, so us boys made a big thing about shaking hands and slapping backs and looking mean and moody. It was a chance sent from heaven to show off. You could see the girls picking out which fellas they fancied. This was a near hundred-strong young mob and our pride and sense of achievement was high that we had pulled so many people together. A few of the black kids from the Suite showed up, making it a brilliant turn-out. Most of the kids on show were from around our neighbourhood; the famous faces were yet to arrive.

It wasn't long before the Old Bill turned up and told us to move along as we were causing an obstruction to the footpath. They always trotted out the same old crap: 'Come on, lads, let's keep it moving, the nice people of Thornton Heath want to go about their business.'

We crossed the road and brought the traffic in both directions to a halt. I could see the sneers on the motorists' faces as we wove in and out of the traffic. 'Bloody yobs,' they were thinking and, in some cases, mouthing. 'A spell in the army would do them good, bloody useless troublemakers.'

A vicar dressed in his white straw hat and dog-collar poked his head out of the car window to see why the traffic had come to a standstill. Sitting next to him in the passenger seat was a middle-aged lady.

'All right, vicar?' said one of the boys. 'You and your bird going out for the day?'

'It just so happens that this young lady is my new organist, and I am on the way to the church to show her my organ,' he replied.

The woman realised what the vicar had just said and burst out laughing.

From the station we heard the biggest roar and chants of '*Chelsea! Chelsea! Chelsea!*' as a trainload of our boys arrived and emerged from the station, spilling out onto the street. Eccles was at the front with the Webb brothers on either side of him. I couldn't believe it – the General had turned up to our meet! Maybe it was just a coincidence. Well, it was his meet now, as he pushed his way to the front and we fell in behind the illustrious new arrivals. I felt exhilarated. I was on my home patch striding down the high street in a massive skinhead mob. The feeling of power was intoxicating. At times like this you felt you could do almost anything. Invade Poland or even Germany. Scare shoppers, motorists and vicars. Then it occurred to me that one of these shoppers could well be my old lady, and my sense of well-being momentarily subsided. I could just imagine her barging past Eccles and co, grabbing me by the ear and shouting, 'What d'you think you're doing walking in the fucking road? Wait till I see your father and tell him the sort of tosspots you're hanging around with! Your feet won't touch the ground!'

A couple of Palace fans with duffle-bags hanging from their shoulders bearing the team's name and colours scurried past but no one touched them. Torment yes, touch no. Duffle-coats and bags were worn by the trainspotting-type football fan and anybody with an ounce of style wouldn't have been seen dead in such things. Maybe 'duffle' is an Old English word for 'naff', I wondered. For years the ever-decreasing duffle-coat brigade had stood on the terraces of football grounds drinking from their thermos flasks, a transistor radio pressed up against their lugholes while they listened to endless reports from other grounds. Team changes were announced over the tannoy and a programme would be quickly pulled from a pocket and the necessary alterations carried out in biro. During the rest of the week the programme would be studied as the fan lay on top of his bed at home and every morsel of information would be digested and remembered. It was hard work being a bore. Almost overnight this type was almost squeezed out of football by gangs of marauding young men and boys with cropped hair and bovver boots.

We headed towards the ground in a mob that must have been touching nearly six hundred-strong. Palace fans in their claret-and-blue scarves saw us coming and darted up side streets or ducked into the nearest shop. Home-owners come out into their gardens and stood defiantly by their front gates. There was no way this mob was going to be allowed to trample their well-tended gardens or raid their larders. Chest out, back straight, 'I was in Monty's Desert Rats and we stood up to the Germans, so the likes of you don't bother me,' I could see they were thinking. An Englishman's home is his castle. 'Good on ya, pops,' we called.

We reached a sign outside the ground that read HOME SUPPORTERS ONLY but we took no notice and started to push through. One bloke realised there was no Old Bill on the other side so he leapt over the metal turnstile. 'Good idea,' everyone thought, and soon we were all doing the same despite the appeals of the man behind the wire collecting the money. I cleared the turnstile in one leap and ran up the concrete steps and out onto the large open terrace. The police came rushing towards me and I froze to the spot, bracing myself for the inevitable arm-up-the-back routine. To my surprise, they carried on past me and headed down the steps to the turnstiles where the Chelsea supporters were still fighting with each other to get through without paying. I'd been here before, the last time to see Man United play, and their fans literally pulled the main gates off their hinges and thousands steamed in without paying. No wonder Palace never buy any decent players, I thought. No one pays to get in so they don't have any money.

On the Holmesdale end terrace I tried to push through and get as near to the middle as I could. The middle was the place to be. It was the same in the Shed at Chelsea – you would always try to get as near to the centre as you could. It didn't matter that you could see fuck all that was going on down on the pitch. It was the thrill of standing in that sea of bodies, telling your mates back home that you watched the whole match from the middle of the Shed. You wanted to get as intense an experience as you could.

As I ducked, squeezed and elbowed my way through the crowd, I saw loads of familiar faces. Chelsea fans filled near enough the whole end and they soon began to sing and chant just to let everyone know who was in control. There was no sign yet of the threatened Palace show. Thousands of Chelsea fans were packed into the White Horse Lane end of the ground, which was designated for away support only, but still more continued to flow in. When they heard us singing in the opposite end hundreds spilled over the small perimeter wall which went round the edge of the pitch and ran across to join us. We applauded wildly, and the more we cheered the more fans poured over the wall towards us. We learned later that Chelsea fans had taken a leaf from the United supporters' book and prised open the gates and shoved in *en masse* and *gratis*.

I saw Eccles being led away by two burly policeman down the side of the pitch. Fans, some of whom were in wheelchairs, sneered comments as the two policemen slowed down to let a photographer take a snapshot. A Palace youth in a felt trilby hat and fake sheepskin jacket watched Eccles' every move, no doubt telling his mate standing next to him what he'd do if he and Eccles were to meet up one night in a dark alleyway. I saw Eccles about five minutes later in our end, so he'd obviously been slung out for not paying, walked around the ground on the outside and paid to get in this time. You can't keep a good man down.

At half-time we ambled up to the tea bar where words were being exchanged between a few older Palace fans and some young Chelsea skins. 'Run along now, Chelsea, you're just dopey little kiddies,' said one.

Another was altogether more aggressive and was confident that because he was older, maybe mid-twenties, he was in the driving seat. He stepped forward towards the group of Chelsea boys and they backed off a bit. They looked around for some support but the older lot were unaware of what was going on and stood around chatting further down the terraces.

'Come on, boys, what's the matter – ain't there enough of you?'

The Palace fan and his mates were gaining confidence from the Chelsea boys' unwillingness to take them on, so they took another two paces forward. I had a good look at this crowd to see if our friends from the fair were in among them but sadly there was no such luck. This lot were even older than the rabble from the fair.

Suddenly, out of the corner of my eye, I saw Jeff standing next to the Palace big mouth and I knew he was going to do something. Jeff's actions no longer surprised me. The Palace bloke slapped a kid almost as young as me and then kicked him up the arse as the boy disappeared into the crowd. He was crying as he held his cheek. He looked more embarrassed than hurt, and I doubted we'd be seeing him with the mob again. Old Big Gob looked like he was about to take on the world and he started to call anyone who fancied a fight towards him. 'Come on, Chelsea,' he tried to say, but only the word 'come' made it out of his mouth as Jeff leapt on his back and some-one else chucked a hot cup of tea in his face. At this we jumped and climbed all over him until he sank to his knees. We were the original Ant Hill Mob.

As expected, his mates melted into the background. He stopped struggling and fell forward as we gleefully kicked and stamped all over his body and head. A couple of policemen shouted and ran across the back of the terrace towards us, holding onto their helmets to stop them falling off. (What fool designed police helmets? They're the most impractical thing for a man of action to wear.) Everyone scarpered. When they picked up the Palace fan he was conscious, tea was dripping from his hair, his face was scratched and bruised and nearly all the buttons were missing from his shirt. An ambulance man who looked like a right child-molester came over and led the bloke away. By the look of it he was still in a daze and he couldn't speak. I almost felt sorry for him but I quickly came to my senses.

During the second half the word was passed around that the 'boys are going shopping'. I didn't understand what this meant but I was soon to find out. At the end of the game we followed the crowds out of the gates, down some side streets where wing mirrors were pulled or kicked off cars and then smashed. A stone was thrown through a front-room window and dustbins were kicked over and the rubblish strewn across the pavement. The mob swarmed out onto the main shopping street and we could hear the sound of breaking glass all around us. Being in the middle of the mob we couldn't see the destruction that was going on. The Old Bill arrived and tried to break the mob up. I saw one kid getting attacked by a police dog. He fell to the ground, clutching his ripped trouser-leg. The dog wrapped its jaws around the kid's neck but the handler reacted quickly and pulled the dog away before it could inflict any serious damage. It was okay to let the dog draw blood but you couldn't very well let it kill people. The copper patted his dog and smiled before moving on to his next victim. How satisfying police work must be.

The crowd broke into a canter and it was clear the boys at the front of the mob were doing some serious damage. We passed a sports shop with all its windows smashed in and what was left of its goods strewn across the pavement. The same had happened to a small off-licence a few doors down. The place looked like it had been nearly emptied. A ladies' dress shop had been smashed up and a full-size naked dummy lay spreadeagled across the path. A man, probably the shop owner, knelt by its side, nearly in tears as he talked to the plastic figure. 'The bastards, they're worse than animals,' he said as he gently laid its head back down onto the pavement and told a passing policeman that he'd had loads of stuff nicked. Who'd want to go around half-inching women's clothes, I wondered. Perhaps the old girl was there after all and she'd loaded up with a new hat and some outfits for the bingo.

I didn't actually see anyone carrying anything that looked like it could have been nicked from the shops, so I wasn't too sure what the 'going shopping' bit was all about. It seemed to me that the objective was just to smash the shops up. I couldn't really see the point – especially on your own doorstep. A lot of the local kids with us used these shops every day of the week.

The vandalism didn't stop there, though. The police eventually herded us on to a couple of waiting trains which they said would take us non-stop through to London. When we pointed out we were local, they replied, 'Tough. You go where we send you.' As soon as the trains pulled away from the platform the destruction started again. First the seats were ripped out and thrown out of the windows, then the lightbulbs were unscrewed and smashed. Next, the mirrors were kicked in and the toilets and sinks torn from the walls. Call me old-fashioned but I couldn't really understand what it was all about. What had the train done to deserve this? It didn't support Palace. It didn't support anyone, as far as I knew.

Suddenly the train screeched to a halt. Some bright spark had pulled the communication cord. Three of the Pollards Hill boys casually opened the door and jumped down onto the embankment. I looked out of the window and could see we were just short of Streatham Common station.

'This will do us,' laughed one. 'We only live up the road.'

'So do we,' thought Jeff and I and we jumped down onto the sidings and followed. We scrambled up the steep bank, climbed through the wire fence and jumped on a bus to Mitcham.

On the bus we sat in complete silence reflecting on the day's events. No one actually said it but I had come to the conclusion that there were two strands of football 'boys' – those who wanted to defend, and those who set out to destroy. I made my mind up to stick with the boys who liked a row and not to knock about with the morons who liked to participate in mass vandalism. I had rationalised that it was okay to punch someone on the nose, but I drew the line at smashing things up just for smashing's sake.

FOUR

The Sky Blues, Blues

Coventry City. It didn't quite have the same ring to it as Man United, Liverpool or Newcastle. Its only claims to fame were its funny-shaped cathedral, Jimmy Hill's funny-shaped chin and that during the Second World War it was the country's most bombed city after London. The football team didn't have much to offer either.

One day we were playing football over at the rec when some older boys from over Tooting junction way joined in. After the game we all sat round talking football: what games we'd been to, what rival fans we'd run, what mobs were up for it – all the usual bullshit.

'If there's one game you should definitely go to this season, make it Coventry away in a few weeks' time,' said Mark, one of the lads from Tooting who had become a bit of a face over at Chelsea. 'It'll go off big time. There'll be fucking murders up there, especially after what happened last season.'

'What happened?' one of us asked.

Mark told us the story. 'Last year we took their end without too much trouble. You know, the usual thing – a mob of us go in, sing "Chelsea" and the end clears. It's so easy – they never put up a fight. Most of the Midlands teams are the same – no bottle. After the game the bulk of us walked back to the station, but about twenty or so lads decided to hang around the ground and wait for a pub to open. After about half an hour they stumbled across a pub down a little back street. They got chatting to the bloke behind the bar but after half an hour boredom had set in. "Why don't you go to the disco pub?" he suggested to them. "It's packed with crumpet and they play all the latest reggae sounds, and it's only a ten-minute stroll up the road. If I wasn't working tonight, I'd be there myself. You should see the fanny up there – they come from all over the Midlands just to find some new blokes. You're near enough guaranteed a bunk-up. In fact, two of my mates pulled a couple of birds there last week and they both shagged them in an alleyway beside the pub."

'The Chelsea boys were all up for it – good music, beer and birds – what more could they want? They drank up and the barman started to give them directions. "I'll tell you what," he says, "I'll give my mate at the pub a ring, let him know you're coming. He works on the door so you'll have no trouble getting in."

'Everyone headed for the door and wished their new friend all the best, with promises to return the following season. As they left, the barman picked up the phone and called his mate. It was cold now, so the Chelsea lads pulled their collars up and hurried along the street, all excited about what was lying in store for them. "Here we are," said one of the lads at the front, "here's the boozer." The pace picked up and their brisk walk nearly turned into a trot. As they approached the front doors of the pub a man standing outside disappeared quickly into the pub. Seconds later, what seemed like an explosion of slow-motion bodies came piling out of the pub and the Chelsea boys ground to a halt. Their attackers were armed to the teeth. Bottles and glasses rained down on our boys. It was a right set-up. Half the Chelsea boys backed off and ran while the other half tried to stand and fight. It was toe-to-toe stuff, but all around people were being felled with whacks from cricket bats and lumps of wood. A Coventry geezer was swinging a baseball bat around his head.

'In the end all our lot had to take off and were chased round the Coventry back streets. The Old Bill turned up and attended to a couple of the lads who were laid out sparko on the floor. Two of them were kept in hospital overnight and the rest were rounded up and escorted back to the station,' finished Mark.

'When Chelsea played Coventry at home this season,' his mate continued, 'as expected only about half a dozen Coventry fans made the trip to Stamford Bridge. But the away game would be different:

thousands of our boys would be heading up there, many with thoughts of revenge uppermost in their minds.'

Sitting there and listening to their tale, we were all up for it, and as usual many of my mates said to count them in for the trip. I knew the game was not for a few weeks and a lot of boys from the park would by then have found reasons not to go or would have simply forgotten about it by then.

After our game of football a few of us headed for Hadfields Park, which was between Mitcham and Morden. It was a large park which had cattle and horses grazing in it. It also had the River Wandle flowing through it, which ended up in Wandsworth, where it flowed into the Thames down by the Youngs brewery. After a game of football on a hot day, a few of us usually headed over to the Wandle to have a dip and cool off with a swim. We'd walk through Phipps Bridge estate, a large council estate with tower blocks. Behind the estate was a smaller group of houses known locally as 'Redskin Village'. It supposedly acquired that name during the Second World War, when the visiting Canadian and American soldiers set up camp there. They erected what the locals said looked like teepees – hence the name Redskin Village. The other version I'd heard was that if you were a stranger and the locals caught you, you'd be scalped. That's the one I tended to believe. It must have been one of the roughest estates in south London. If you had two ears you were looked upon as a sissy.

After our swim in the cold, dark-brown, smelly water, we sat around and dried off in the sun. A couple of girls we knew from the estate stopped and chatted. 'You lot going to Merton Hall tonight?' they asked.

'Why? What's happening there?'

'There's a dance down there, and quite a few girls from Willows School are going.'

Willows Girls' School was in Morden, so a lot of the talent there was unknown to us – we only mixed with girls from our school or the odd bird picked up at the fair, so the chance to mix and blagg something new appealed to us. They gave us all the details.

'We'll meet you there, then, girls,' I said as we jumped to our feet and headed off home to get ready. No need to have a bath or a wash: the cleansing, therapeutic water of the River Wandle was my scrub-up. (How we never got infected with some horrible disease I'll never know. Perhaps, like the women of Mitcham, we learned not to swallow.)

'Call for you at seven,' said Tony as he left me at the corner of my street. I had a quick go at bowling one of the Ballard brothers out as they played cricket in the middle of the road using the Rodney Road sign as the stumps. I bowled Fatty Ballard, the youngest of the Ballard piglets, a leg-spinner. 'Howzat!' I shouted as the ball thumped against the brick wall holding the road sign. 'See ya later, boys,' I said, 'I'm off in search of the fur burger.'

The Ballard kids looked at one another blankly. They were too young to be really interested in girls and I guessed they would prefer a big dinner to shagging a bird. 'Bet they've never even had a hard-on before,' I thought to myself.

I let myself in through the front door, and bounded straight up the stairs two at a time.

'Don't get in the hot bath I've just run!' shouted my brother from the foot of the stairs.

'You're fucking joking! Him, have a bath!' I heard my mum laughing.

I hauled the wardrobe doors open and surveyed the piles of creased clothes just slung at the bottom. Empty hangers with nothing on them stared back at me. I made a mental note that in future I would hang things up. I found a Brutus green-and-yellow check button-down shirt. 'Fuck, it'll have to do,' I thought. 'I ain't in the mood for poncing about.'

'Mum!' I yelled over the banisters. 'Any chance of ironing a shirt for me?'

Complete silence.

Back in my room, I stripped down to my socks and pants and looked in my drawers for some clean replacements. Nothing, fuck all, the drawers were all empty. 'Fuck it, the pants and socks I've got on will have to do,' I told myself. As I pulled on my white Sta-prest, I noticed a small grass stain on one of the knees – or could it be dog-shit? It must have happened playing football over at the park. I pulled the trousers off again and took them into the bathroom. I dipped my brother's flannel in his hot soapy bath water and rubbed ferociously on the stain. After a few seconds it faded. Thank fuck for that. It must have been dogshit because grass wouldn't come off that easily. I dropped the flannel back into the water and it sank to the bottom. I left the trousers to dry next to the small gas fire and shouted again from the top of the stairs, 'Mum, any chance of ironing a shirt for me?'

'All right, all right, you impatient little bastard, throw it down,' she said, appearing at the bottom of the stairs. She picked up the shirt and looked up at me. 'I see the bullworker your dad brought you is working,' she laughed as she turned and walked away.

I checked myself in the bathroom mirror, puffing my chest out. 'Fuck all happens, it still looks the same,' I said to myself. I did a couple of bodybuilder poses and checked myself in the mirror again. My mother was definitely taking the piss. I was no Charles Atlas – more like Charles Hawtrey, the puny geezer with the goggles out of the *Carry On* films.

I splashed on some Brut, pulled on my trousers and went down-stairs to find Mum hadn't even started to iron my shirt yet. 'Come on, Ma,' I moaned. 'I'm waiting to go out.'

'I'm waiting for the bleedin' iron to warm up,' she said, not taking her eyes off the telly. My brother and dad were glued to it too. 'What a fucking family,' I thought. 'The world could be ending and my mob are glued to *Crossroads*, the sad TV soap story of everyday life in a motel somewhere in the Midlands made for even sadder people who sit glued to it five nights a week.'

The doorbell rang and it was Tony.

'You ready, Kingy?'

'Yeah, I'll just grab my shirt and I'll be right with ya,' I told him.

He followed me up the hallway and into the front room.

'Hello, Tone,' said the old girl, not taking her eyes from the flickering black-and-white screen. 'Your mum gone to the bingo tonight?' she asked.

'Yes,' said Tony, 'the old man's walked up there with her and he'll wait till she comes out and then walk back home with her.'

Mum smiled. 'I don't think he's going to hang about outside for her. He'll probably wait in the King's Head opposite and have a few brown and milds.'

'True love,' I said scornfully, 'isn't it wonderful?'

The old girl quickly rubbed my shirt over with the iron and I slipped it on.

'I suppose you've had a hot bath today, Tony?' asked the old girl.

'Oh, yeah, yeah,' he muttered.

'Like fuck,' chipped in Dad, 'him and all his mates are right fuckin' soap-dodgers. A few years in the army would straighten them out. It didn't do me no harm. Teaches you self-discipline and hygiene, turns you from a boy into a man. You learn how to look after yourself, how to cope.'

'Yeah, right, Dad,' I said. 'Anyway, I thought that the Germans and the British went to war and they hated one another.'

'That's right, son,' said the old man, 'and we won. We knocked the stuffing right out of the Gerry bastards.'

'Then, Dad,' I asked, 'why did you end up marrying Hitler's sister?'

The old girl made out she was going to throw the iron at me. 'Go on, fuck off out of it, you cheeky pair of gits!' she shouted, and Tony and I were out of the door like rockets.

'Who's going to the disco tonight?' I asked when we were safely out of reach.

'Looks like just me and you. I went round for Jeff and he's going to the pub with his dad. Nicky and Seamus are both babysitting for their younger brothers and sisters, so it looks like there will be all the more birds for us two!'

We decided to walk instead of catching a bus, taking a shortcut along the old disused railway track between Mitcham and south Wimbledon. Climbing over the wooden fence we both got dirt and grease on our hands and trousers. We weren't there yet and we were both rotten dirty.

'Whose fucking idea was it to come this way?' grumbled Tony, rubbing his hands together to try to get some of the grease off.

'Yours, I think, Tone,' I replied.

We crossed the railway track and climbed out the other side on to the main road. Happy memories of a cup final came flooding back as we passed the field where my junior school, Benedict, won the borough under-elevens challenge cup. What a day! We celebrated like we'd just won the FA Cup. Who says you need alcohol to enjoy yourself?

When we reached Merton Hall, we saw that there was already quite a crowd queuing for the doors to open. The disco was supposed to be for under-sixteens but we spotted a lad from Mitcham called Sammy who was knocking on thirty if he was a day. With him were his brothers, Lenny and Freddie, who were our age and who were looked up to by a few of the local herberts. They'd been in and out of Borstal for the last few years so some of our mob saw them as some sort of heroes. They were from a large family – there were thirteen children, I think – and on Guy Fawkes night one year their street made a huge bonfire with old furniture on the nearby playing-field. All the kids were stacking the bonfire nice and high. Sammy and his clan, meanwhile, were dragging off wardrobes and other bits of furniture and mattresses and carrying them home before they were burnt.

I'd been over to their house one night when their mum had sent the youngest brother, Ringo, to the fish-and-chip shop. He returned and tipped out a large bag of chips and half a dozen Saveloys straight on to the table. No knives and forks or plates for this lot – everyone just tucked in. They even took it in turns to swig from a large bottle of Tizer. I sat there dumbfounded, never having seen anything like it.

Sammy was one of the older ones and, being just a little bit simple, mixed with teenagers like us. He was a compulsive liar and told all us kids that he'd played football for Chelsea, was George Best's closest friend, had been a good boxer, winning an Olympic gold medal before turning pro, represented Britain in ice-skating and small-bore shooting. Every time he saw a girl he'd say, 'I've shagged her,' and he reckoned he had fathered untold numbers of kids. I certainly never met any of them. Now and again you'd see him pushing a pram through Mitcham, not with a baby in it, but loaded up with lead or copper he'd just pinched off a roof somewhere. And he was shy of a day's work – I don't think he'd ever done one in his life. His most amusing habit was that he called everyone he met by the name Chris. 'Hello, Chris', 'See ya, Chris', 'All right, Chris', 'Speak to ya later, Chris'. Even people he'd known for years he still called Chris.

The bouncers arrived and the doors were opened. They nodded to Sammy and his brothers. The long queue began to shuffle slowly inside as flashing lights and the sound of Desmond Dekker blasted out of the massive speakers on either side of the stage. The place was packed with plenty of crumpet on parade, some of which we'd not seen before.

We queued to buy a drink. There wasn't much of a choice – Coke, lemonade or Tizer, nothing stronger. Groups of boys hung around chatting and watching the girls dance. The boys from Mitcham stood in one corner, the Wimbledon boys in another, the Tooting lads stood around the bar, and the bouncers, knowing if there was any real trouble they'd have it under control in seconds, stood near by. It was only kids they were supervising, but they still kept a close eye on the uneasy peace. Tony and I struck up a conversation with a lad we knew from Morden who had a Chelsea scarf round his neck. We'd seen him over at the Wyvern youth club, where us Mitcham boys were not very welcome. There was a lot of rivalry between the two gangs. But we had one thing in common and that was Chelsea.

'Going to Coventry?' I shouted above the music.

'You bet!' he shouted back, 'I won't be missing that one.' A few of his mates crowded around and joined in. 'This lot are all going,' he told us.

'Right!' we said, nodding to each and every one of them.

'Fucking hell, Tone,' I said, 'there's a right mob heading north in a few weeks' time.'

'Looks like it,' said Tony. 'Let's hope we've got some money to be able to go. That's the trouble with being at school – you've got no regular income. Still, we can always go out with Sammy and his pram.'

The night before the game, our lot met over the rec. Tony, Jeff and I were the only ones who would be heading north to Coventry in the morning. The others, as usual, had bottled out or were skint.

Half seven at Jeff's house was the meet. I even shocked Mum by being in bed by the time she came back from the bingo. I tossed and turned all night and it seemed that I hardly had a wink of sleep.

When the old man's alarm clock went off, I heard him get up and open my bedroom door. 'It's half six, boy,' he called.

'Righto, Dad,' I said, 'I'll be down in a minute.' As I lay there for another five minutes in my nice warm bed, it crossed my mind to give the football a miss but I realised I would be as bad as all the other no-shows who said they were going to turn up every week.

I jumped out of bed, the cold frosty morning air making me rush to get dressed. I slipped on my trousers over the pants and socks I'd worn in bed that night. I put on my shirt and jumper and began to lace up my Dr Marten boots. I could hear the old man downstairs lighting and stoking up the morning fire. The kettle whistled and I heard the sound of water being poured into the teapot. The old man was off to work and I was off to do my paper round. Today was payday for me, so I would have some money for football. I ran the cold-water tap and splashed my face, brushed my teeth and flicked some Brut behind my ears. I passed Dad on the stairs as he carried up a tray with Mum's tea and toast on it. 'See you later, Pa,' I said, 'I'm going straight to the football when I finish my paper round. It's up at

Coventry so I won't be back till late, so can you walk the dog?' Usually our old dog Rex came with me on my paper round.

Dad dipped in his back pocket and pulled out two crisp green one-pound notes. 'There you go, son,' he said, with a smile. 'Give it back if you don't spend it.'

'Cheers, Dad!' I said. I was at an age now where I didn't know how to thank him. Did I shake his hand or give him a kiss on the cheek? 'Cheers, Dad,' I said again, not sure how to end the conversation.

'Behave yourself, boy,' shouted Mum as the front door slammed behind me.

I delivered all my papers in double-quick time. I didn't even bother to read the back pages I was in such a hurry to get finished.

I collected my wages and headed for Jeff's house. Tony was already there, stuffing a whole slice of toast in his mouth at once.

'Right, let's go,' said Jeff, 'Coventry, here we come!'

We made our way to the other side of London and into Euston Station. Hundreds and hundreds of the chaps were there already. We bought our tickets and stood around with the rest of the shaven-headed youths who didn't seem to know quite what to do next.

'Who are we all waiting for?' I asked Jeff.

'Probably Eccles or Greenaway,' he replied.

'Why are we waiting for them?'

'Because they're the main boys.'

I was still none the wiser so Jeff started to explain. 'It's like an army,' he told me. 'You've got your colonels and sergeants and without them the troops don't know what to do or what positions to take up. It's the same with a football mob: someone's got to make the decisions. Someone's got to lead from the front. The leaders are not just the best fighters but also the best organisers.'

'And what are we?' said Tony. 'The infantry?'

'No, we're the catering corps,' I laughed as I counted how many Mars Bars I'd nicked from the paper shop that morning.

'Shut up, you two piss-takers,' said Jeff.

People were starting to move towards a platform as word got

around that Eccles had just turned up with his small band of hench-men and we were about to depart.

British Rail had laid on one of its football specials and, by the look of its carriages, Stephenson's *Rocket* had once pulled them along. We met up with some of the lads from Tooting and talked excitedly about what lay ahead. Those who'd been caught out in the ambush the previous year were supposedly on the train, and rumour had it one of them had a machete and was going to cut off a Coventry fan's ear and take it home as a souvenir.

'Wait till they hear about that at school on Monday,' I thought. 'Perhaps the bloke with the machete would let me borrow the ear to show my mates. What a shock they'd have. I can just see it now: every-one crowding around in the science lab to see what I have in the matchbox that I've just pulled from my pocket. I slide open the box and inside is the severed ear. Dried blood congealed around where it has been sliced from the side of the victim's head. Two kids faint as I remove a tiny piece of wax from inside the earlobe . . . "Scruffy northern bastard," I'd say, "you'd think he'd have a wash before he set off to football!" '

The train rumbled into Coventry and as usual everyone was off before it came to a halt. Noise echoed around the high-roofed station as a chant of '*Chelsea*' rose up. There was no Old Bill to meet us and everyone headed for the main exit. We were out onto the street. 'This looks like a good tight mob,' I thought, 'one that knows what it's come here for.'

'Stick together!' someone shouted A cheer went up as someone knocked the head off a stone statue. More cheers followed as a phone box was smashed and the coin box looted.

'Right here!' someone shouted. 'Straight on!', 'Right here!', 'Left here!' The mob moved menacingly along as one.

There were no pubs open – it was far too early in the day for that. A copper on a bike asked someone at the front where they're off to. 'Pictures,' was the reply. Everyone laughed and the copper cycled off.

'Left here! Right here!' Fuck me, how much farther? My feet were aching already.

'Let's get up to the front,' said Jeff.

A park came into view and we could see a football match going on. The players spotted us and took off in every direction. The mob ripped the goalposts down and tore the nets to pieces. We climbed over the fence at the other side of the park and momentarily the mob came to halt.

'We're lost,' someone said, so it was back across the park. A few of the scattered players were trying to put the goalposts back up, until they saw us coming back and they were on their toes again.

'Right, let's start again,' said someone at the front and we got under way and moved off. 'Left here, right here, left here, straight on.'

A big cheer of relief went up as we suddenly saw the floodlights.

'Look, there's Stamford Bridge,' someone laughed. The amount of miles we'd walked, it could well be.

A few Old Bill appeared but just stood back and watched. It looked like they were not really that interested.

'Let's find this pub where their boys drink,' said one of our faces, ever eager for confrontation.

'Let's just get in any pub,' came back the reply. 'After the game we'll go looking for this boozer.'

Everyone agreed. The first pub we came to was overrun with our lot. We stood outside and after ten minutes we decided to go and have a look around.

'Come on,' said Jeff, 'let's go and feed our faces.' In all the excitement we'd forgotten our hunger. Something nice and greasy would do. We found a café and stuffed our faces with sausage, egg, chips and beans, and gave the pinball machine a good hammering. Some Coventry fans our age came in, looked around and walked out. It must have been their usual haunt but they probably felt put out with us lot in there.

As it got close to kick-off time, the pubs, which were full of Chelsea fans, began to empty. We left the café and headed towards the ground. The word on the street before the game was that we would take the Coventry end of the ground. We queued for the home end terraces and paid to go in, unchallenged by the coppers standing by the turnstiles. The odd few Coventry fans protested to the Old Bill about us invading their end, but the police weren't interested. This part of the stadium was already three-quarters full and by the look of it the majority were Chelsea fans. The teams were announced over the tannoy and every Coventry player's name was met with a loud boo or catcall. I looked around and was thrilled at the number of Chelsea boys in this end.

The Chelsea team was announced to loud cheers. 'Chelsea, Chelsea!' everyone around me chanted. The duffle-coats with the flasks and the anoraks at the front behind the goal joined in.

When the teams came out, a small pocket of Coventry fans to our right cheered their players on to the field. 'Come on, City! come on, City!' they chanted.

'Fuck off, City! Fuck off, City!' chanted our lot back. A scuffle broke out and the Old Bill moved in and ejected the fifty or so Coventry fans. How humiliating! As they were led round the pitch to the safety of the other end of the ground, we wondered how they must have felt. Their home end had been completely overrun by Chelsea fans. We sarcastically waved farewell to them. As the police led them away, they didn't even look back. They got a few wolf-whistles from our lot and shouts of 'see you later, girls' as they disappeared into the other end of the ground.

There was no more trouble during the game but at the final whistle the Chelsea hordes poured out onto the streets. The Old Bill were powerless to stop our mob heading towards a pub which had Coventry fans waiting outside. They were quickly chased away and our attention was diverted to a group of about twenty Coventry fans waiting at a bus-stop. They were surrounded, punched and kicked, and their sky-blue-and-white scarves ripped from their necks. We tied them to our belts and hung them down our sides like some kind of trophy.

The City fans along the way soon got wise and gave us a wide berth. Anyone not quick enough was kicked out of the way. We walked for what felt like miles. The pub we were looking for was supposed to be this way and we'd all turn right. Next it was that way and we'd all turn left. Five minutes later someone shouted, 'It's this way!' and off we went again.

Some of the boys were getting fed up and the word went round that the next pub we came to was going to get hit big time. Sure enough, a pub was attacked and the windows were smashed in but our mob was so large that by the time we got to it the Old Bill had arrived and started arresting people, so we missed most of the action. The police had seen enough and pushed everyone in the direction of the train station.

'That'll let those Coventry wankers know that the Chelsea boys have been in their city,' I heard a tall skinhead say to his mate as he stuffed a beer mat, nicked from the trashed pub, into his Crombie pocket.

'Fucking hell!' I thought. 'What a hero! He lives dangerously. Wait till he shows off his Coventry beer mat to his mates back home in London. What a prize! Wanker! What's the point of smashing up a pub when there's no one inside it?'

Back at the station we were herded on to a train. Everyone looked knackered with all the walking. It was time to reflect on the day's events and, in all honesty, it had been a bit of an anticlimax.

I fell sleep and woke up a couple of times. Tony and Jeff were sound asleep. I drifted off again and woke as the train came to a standstill at Euston.

Back home, I pulled my boots and socks off and warmed my feet by the glowing coal fire.

'Good day?' asked the old man.

'Yeah, not bad,' I replied, and before long was back in the land of nod.

FIVE

Brass Monkeys

'Open the front door for your dad, will ya, boy!' shouted Mum as the old man struggled to open the door with his key and keep his bike upright.

'Here, Dad, let me take the bike,' I said.

He stamped the sleet off his boots onto the doormat and pulled his gloves off. He took a hanky from his trouser pocket and wiped the dew drop hanging from his nose. 'Fucking freezing out there,' he said as he unwrapped the ten-foot-long woollen scarf from around his neck. 'That scarf's the best Christmas present your nan's ever knitted.' He took his coat off. 'You ain't going to the football in this weather, are ya, boy?' he asked.

'No, the Fulham game's been called off, I've just heard the announcement on the radio,' I told him.

'What about the Chelsea game up at Burnley?'

'Yeah, that's still on,' I said. 'They were saying on the radio it would probably be the match of the day. Good side, Burnley. Got some decent players. Got a good support, too, home and away. I suppose there's fuck all else to get excited about up there except follow the football team. Still, it's the same with all those northern teams – it's either work, if you're lucky enough to have a job, or football.'

Mum interrupted. 'Mart, can you run up to the baker's in Edmund Road and get us some crusty rolls for your dad's lunch? And while you're there, could you pop next door to the sweetshop and get us some fags?' she said sweetly and disappeared back into the kitchen.

I took my Crombie from the bottom banister where it had hung all night. 'What fags do you want?' I shouted to the kitchen.

'Sh, sh,' said Mum, coming out into the hall and putting her finger to her lips, 'your brother's in bed. Don't wake him up, for God's sake.'

Fucking good, ain't it. It was one o'clock in the afternoon and my brother was still in his pit, fast asleep. He probably didn't get in till midday, come to think of it. I didn't notice him in when I got up at six to do my paper round. 'I expect he'll wake up about five o'clock tonight, take over the bathroom for two or three hours, get himself all spruced up and then back out on the piss again,' I muttered to myself. I opened the front door and there was a blizzard blowing outside.

'Hurry up, boy, don't dawdle,' said Mum almost pushing me out the door.

The driving sleet hit me in the face and it stung and hurt. The biting wind rushed down the back of my neck and up the sleeves of my coat, freezing my hands and my ankles after only a few steps. I wanted to turn back. What would be worse? The cold and wet or my Mum's tongue? I carried on. Already my feet were soaked through. 'Scott of the Antarctic, I know how you felt, mate! What mother sends her child out in weather like this? She says if the school board catches me bunking off school, she'll be sent to prison. So what would they do to her for sending me out in conditions like this?' I wondered.

I reached the shops, my hands numb with the cold. I pulled off one glove just to check my fingers were all there and that my hand was still connected to my wrist.

'Hello, Martin,' said Dolly, the woman who worked in the baker's. 'What the hell are you doing out on a day like this? You should be shot.'

'Take yer gun around to my house,' I told her, 'and shoot my mum, because she's the one who sent me out.'

Dolly smiled. I took the brown paper bag of rolls and stuffed them inside my Crombie.

'Go straight home, boy!' said Dolly.

I headed next door to Mr Patel's to get the old girl her fags. I decided to treat myself to a comic out of the change – she wouldn't notice and even if she did, she was hardly likely to go storming up to the shop in this weather. I wanted to make her pay for chucking me out in these Arctic conditions. Why didn't she go up to the shops herself? Too fucking lazy, that's why.

'Hello, Martin, my good friend,' said Mr Patel. 'What brings you out on a day like today?' Everyone was Mr Patel's good friend, he greeted everyone the same way.

'It's not what brings me out,' I replied, 'it's more like what's chucked me out.'

'Okay, my good friend, what can I get you?'

'Twenty of those fags the old girl smokes.'

He handed them over.

'Lovely weather, Mr Patel,' I said as I tucked Mum's fags deep into my pocket.

'Yes, yes,' he nodded, knowing I was taking the piss, 'go straight home now.'

I pulled the collar on my coat up further and tried to bury my head as far down inside as I could. My ears, stinging with the cold, were nearly resting on the bag containing the rolls. 'Fucking hell, it's cold,' I said to myself. I checked my pockets and for a moment I couldn't feel Mum's packet of fags. *Shit! I've lost them! She'll kill me!* Then the panic was over as I found them in my inside pocket. The cold was numbing my brain.

I carried on up the road towards home, my eyes looking down at the pavement as I tried to avoid the pools of slush. A figure loomed up in front of me. 'Sorry, mate,' I said. I tried to sidestep the overcoat in front of me. I could just about see through my coat's buttonholes, but the overcoat in front of me stepped back into my path. 'Sorry, mate,' I said again and took a step to the right to allow the overcoat to pass. The figure did the same. Now I'd got the hump. I'd no time for silly games.

'For fuck's sake, get out of the fucking way,' I snarled as I popped my head out from under my coat. I clenched my fist as tight as the cold would allow. 'You're going to pay for this!'

Standing there smiling was Tony. 'All right, Kingy,' he said. 'Your mum said she'd sent you up to the shops. Cold, ain't it!'

'No,' I replied. 'It's *fucking* cold.'

'Coming to the football?' he asked.

'You're joking! What football is on in this weather?'

'Tooting and Mitcham are at home.'

'No, fuck it,' I said, 'it's too cold,' and I buried my nut back into my coat. Tony's ears were red and looked like they were almost throbbing with the cold. His nose was running and he lifted the sleeve of his Crombie to wipe the dangling snot. The silver trail on his cuff looked like a snail had crawled along his arm. 'Dirty bastard,' I thought.

We reached my house and I dumped my shopping on the table and stood in front of the fire.

'Cold, innit,' said the old man, his eyes not moving from the horse-racing on the telly. 'Look at that, boy, that's Doncaster on the telly – look at the brilliant sunshine.'

'Yeah,' I nodded, 'it's warmed me up no end just watching it.'

Tony laughed.

'Take your coat off, boy,' said Mum, 'and have some hot soup and one of them crusty rolls you've just brought.'

'No thanks, Ma,' I said, 'I'm going to the football with Tony.'

'Football!' laughed the old man. 'There won't be no football on in this weather, you're fucking mad!'

'Come on,' said Tony, 'it's less than an hour to kick-off.'

'Rene, have a word with your son,' said the old man. 'I think he's going round the twist. He's talking about going out in weather like this to watch football.'

There was nothing Mum could say – after all, I'd just been out running errands for her. No one had mentioned the state of the weather then. The wind howled and you could see the sleet covering the rooftops on the other side of the street. She threw some more coal on the fire. Dad noisily finished his soup.

'Mart, are you coming to the game or not?' said Tony.

'You sure it'll be on?' I asked.

'I'm sure,' he said, 'they'll have covered the pitch with a tarpaulin. I'm sure it'll be on.'

So we went back out the front door and into the driving sleet. 'I must be potty,' I thought to myself.

It was a half-hour walk to Tooting and Mitcham's ground at Sandy Lane and we ran half the way. The sleet by now had turned to snow and was starting to settle and get crisp underfoot.

'There's no way this game's going to be on,' I mumbled.

Tony's hair had turned white with the driving snow. He didn't bother to answer. Perhaps his lips had frozen together. When he took his hands out of his pockets to wipe the snow off his head I noticed his fingers were almost blue with the cold. Pictures of the North Pole, penguins, polar bears, Eskimos, seals, igloos, icebergs, fridges, ice-cream – anything that's cold – came into my mind.

We reached the top of Sandy Lane where usually you would start to see crowds of people heading towards the ground. They weren't a professional team but it wasn't unusual to get a couple of thousand people at home games. There had even been a few full houses in some FA Cup games. Today, though, there was no one. The streets were deserted. When we got to the main gates a handwritten sign was hanging from the rusty Tooting and Mitcham emblem:

GAME OFF. WATER-LOGGED PITCH.

'What happened to the fucking tarpaulin?' I yelled. 'Have they lent it to someone for their leaking shed roof who's forgotten to return it? Fucking tarpaulin!'

Tony said nothing as we headed back the way we'd come. Before long he tried to start a conversation.

'Don't say a word,' I said with an icy glare, 'don't say a fucking word.'

'Sorry,' he said quietly, 'sorry.'

We walked back to my house in complete silence. The only sounds were the howling wind and the noise of our wet feet sliding through semi-frozen water. We reached Gas Works Alley and Tony broke off without a word and headed off towards his house. I carried on. I was angry. 'Why the fuck did I ever go out? I must be mad,' I told myself. I couldn't work out who I was angry with – was it with myself for listening to Tony? Or was I angry with Mum? The only one with any sense seemed to be my brother. He'd the right idea – lie in a nice cosy warm bed all day. He wasn't as daft as he made out.

The cold subsided a little as I turned into the alleyway at the top of my street and then the icy gale blew up again as I walked up the front path. 'It's fucking cold,' I said aloud, 'it's fucking freezing.'

Inside, Mum and Dad were glued to the wrestling on the telly.

'Mick McManus has just beat Jackie Pallo,' said the old man.

I took my coat off and threw it over an empty armchair. I pushed the dog out of the way of the fire with my foot. He looked up at me as if to say 'Oi, I'm sitting here, what did you wake me up for? I was in a deep sleep.' I plonked myself down in his place. 'Sorry, Rex. I must get warm.'

'The big tag match is on next, boy,' said Dad as he popped a boiled sweet into his chops. He could hardly contain his excitement. He loved the wrestling.

'Really,' I replied. 'I'm not interested.'

'Where's your mate gone?' asked Mum. 'I thought you and what's-his-name – you know, him with the funny eyes – were going to watch football. Off to Burnley, weren't you?'

I pulled my soaking wet socks off and watched the steam rise off my toes, which were almost resting on the burning embers.

'I ain't got no mates!' I replied.

SIX

The Carrot-Cruncher

'King! Sit down, will you, lad, and take that smirk off your face!'

The teacher was telling me off for standing up and making the wankers sign out of the back window of the coach taking me and twenty of my classmates to Streatham Ice-Rink. It was all part of a new programme of physical education. We got to escape school for swimming, cycling and rambling and, like today, ice-skating.

All the boys sat at the back of the coach, singing football songs. The girls were down at the front, talking about David Cassidy and Donny Osmond, a couple of right dickheads they'd probably read about in the latest girly magazines – you know the type, loads of adverts for acne lotion and jam rags, and a colour centrefold of the latest teen stars from America. Five minutes later it would be up on their bedroom wall and they'd be swearing undying love for them and camping all night outside some posh London hotel hoping to catch a glimpse of the gleaming white buck-toothed spotty-faced gits. Now and again they would glance at the back of the bus and at us lot with looks of disgust. They thought they were older than they really were – fourteen going on twenty-one, and ugly with it.

'Keep the noise down, lads,' said the teacher, standing up the front of the coach. We came to a stop just outside the front doors of the ice-rink. The teacher stubbed out his cigarette before opening the door to let us off. We clambered over the seats to be the first off. There was no orderly queue.

'There's a good advert for physical education,' I said, pointing to the dog-end smouldering in the ashtray.

'Just get off the coach, King, will you,' growled the PE teacher.

'Don't tell me ya can't read all the signs in the coach that say "No Smoking"! Call yerself a teacher! You can't even read! What chance have we got of learning off someone like you?' I replied cheekily.

'Piss off, King, and get yourself a pair of ice-skating boots inside. Hurry along, lad!' he said, giving me a gentle push so that I fell down the coach steps.

I stopped and turned round to face him, gritting my teeth. 'Fucking wanker,' I muttered under my breath.

Inside it was one mass ruck to get the ice boots. There was no queuing and everyone was shouting out their boot size at the man behind the counter. Eventually, I got my pair and staggered towards the ice. It was near impossible to walk in those things. Kids from other schools were here, so I was trying my best to stay upright.

We'd been coming for a few months by now, so I was not too bad once I was out on the ice. Mick, Bobby and I skated round together, our eyes scanning the horizon for any decent crumpet. Music blared out from the speakers as we skated round in circles, everyone going in the same direction.

All the kids in my class were in their last year of school, so the teachers basically didn't give a fuck. They would take us out on all sorts of trips, just to keep us away from the school grounds, it seemed. A few weeks before they had taken us on a hike from Epsom Downs racecourse to Box Hill. I don't know what the point of such a walk was but it was very long, about ten miles, and all across hilly countryside. I imagine it was to wear us kids out and allow the teachers to get their own back on any pupil who had stepped out of line. It was a difficult walk on a hot sunny day but we loved it, even if we were a little thirsty by the time we reached the end. One or two of the teachers were feeling a bit the worse for wear when we finally reached the top of Box Hill. That last six hundred-foot climb really sorted out the boys from the men. The following day, a couple of teachers failed to show up at school, their excuse being that they had sunstroke and heat exhaustion.

Whenever we'd been out for the day there were never any essays to write the following morning about where we'd been or what we had done. It seemed a bit of a pointless exercise. I wasn't complaining, though. I hated school. School was for people who wanted to learn and educate themselves. I'd learnt to read and write and that was enough for me. I wanted to get out into the big wide world and start earning some serious wedge. The only good thing about going to a mixed school like mine was the chance to look at the girls. To me school was a pain in the arse, a hindrance. Fuck all that messing about with Bunsen burners and litmus paper and adding up figures and fractions. Twenties, tens and pound notes were all I was interested in. I wanted to have money in my pocket and nice clothes, buy a couple of LPs every week and bung the old girl ten bob housekeeping, and maybe go to Bognor for my holidays. That was the life I dreamt of having once I'd left school.

Mick interrupted my daydreaming and pointed out a couple of birds that were looking in our direction. They were sitting down on the other side of the ice-rink. We skated over, trying our best not to go arse over tit.

'Hello, girls,' I yelled, trying to make myself heard above Max Romeo singing about having a wet dream. A 'wet dream'? What the fuck was one of those?

'What did you say?' shouted one of the girls.

'I said, hello, girls.'

'Can't hear you above the music,' said one of the girls, shouting.

'Show us your tits, then,' I said.

'What?' she said, 'I can't hear you.'

Mick and Bob laughed.

'How about giving us a wank, then?'

The girl looked back blankly. 'Sorry, I can't hear you,' she mouthed. The music stopped suddenly. 'That's better, I can hear you now. What did you say?' And she gave me a lovely smile.

'Just hello,' I said, 'and do you come here every week?'

'Come and sit with us,' she said.

We plonked ourselves down next to them and chatted away.

'We've seen you here before,' said the girl. 'I looked out to see if you were here and I spotted your light-green Harrington jacket.'

'Yeah, it is a bit bright,' I said.

'No, it's lovely,' she said and started unzipping it and rubbing her hand inside the lining. 'And I like your Sta-prest trousers, too,' she went on, rubbing the top of my leg.

I could feel the blood rushing to my cory and hoped she wouldn't notice the bulge in my strides. I'd got the popcorn now. 'Do you fancy meeting up for a drink after school?' I asked. How very grown up! The drink would have to be in the Wimpy bar, because there was no way I'd get served in a pub. I wouldn't even know what to ask for.

'Sorry, I've got to go straight home, I've got to go shopping with my mum and sister.'

'What school do you go to?'

'One in Morden.'

'What about tomorrow?'

'I can meet you tomorrow afternoon,' she said.

'I can't,' I said, 'I'm going to watch Chelsea at Stamford Bridge, we've got Norwich in a cup match. You can come if you want.'

Her face lit up at the prospect.

Now that would be something! Martin King turning up at the match with a bird on his arm. I'd take her right into the middle of the Shed. I'd be the envy of every skinhead there. She'd get her bum pinched and squeezed a thousand times. She'd love it. She'd be the centre of attention, the Princess of the Shed. Afterwards, I'd take her over to Mitcham Common and ride the arse off it, or at least get a wank and a bit of tit.

'I've cracked it here,' I thought. 'But hold up a minute, how am I going to pay for her to go to football? There's the train fare, the money to get in, a programme, hotdogs, drinks! I ain't paying for her out of me paper-round money and I can't ask the old man for extra money – how would I explain to him? "Any chance of some more money, Dad, so I can take a tart to football?" He'd laugh his bollocks off! Then he'd tell Mum, who'd give me untold stick, and she'd tell me brother, who'd tell his mates. No, forget it.'

I put my brain into overdrive. 'On second thoughts, love,' I said, 'I think it might be too rough. Perhaps another time?'

'Yeah, okay,' she said disappointedly, and I could tell by her face that she knew I was backtracking.

A whistle blew and it meant everyone had to clear the ice.

'See ya next week,' I said to her.

'Hope so,' she smiled.

Fuck it, I thought, go for it. Her big blue eyes were inviting me to stick my tongue right down her throat. I pulled her towards me and our lips met. Our tongues tangled together and I felt around the inside of her mouth. She didn't have many fillings and her breath didn't smell.

'King! Put that young lady down at once! The coach is waiting, so hurry along!'

Talking of bad breath, trust that arsehole of a teacher to catch me in a clinch.

We parted and she smiled and waved and blew me a kiss.

'She's fucking gorgeous!' I thought. 'See ya next week,' I shouted.

'Come on, King, quickly, you're holding the coach up.'

I boarded the coach and everybody let out a cheer. I strolled casually up the aisle, grinning and winking at everyone. I gave the thumbs-up sign.

'Here's lover boy! Did you shag it?' someone shouted. 'Show us your cory, I bet it's rock hard!'

I felt my face going red. 'Yes, my cory is hard,' I replied.

The girls all sniggered, but to the boys I was one of the chaps.

I gazed out of the window as we drove back through the streets of south London to school.

'You thinking about that bird?' asked Bobby.

'Yeah, lovely, wasn't she? I can't wait until next week. I'm going to ask her out,' I said.

'What's her name?' asked Bob.

I laughed. 'Fucked if I know, I forgot to ask her.'

I was in a daze. That girl was on my mind constantly. 'This is it,' I was thinking. 'I've found the girl of my dreams.'

Back home, I ran straight upstairs and got changed.

'All right, boy?' Mum asked.

'Yeah, I'm going over the park to play football with the boys,' I shouted as I slammed the front door behind me.

Walking to the park, I kicked an empty Coke can along the ground. Usually I'd be a Chelsea player scoring the winning goal in the Cup final, but today there was no daydreaming about football because she was back on my mind. *Wonder if she's a Mandy. No, I bet she's a Tracey. Maybe a Wendy. Could even be a Sue or a Julie.*

When I reached the park, a few of the boys were already having a kickabout. Pear Brewley was running about like a headless chicken. He'd just come out of hospital after breaking his leg in a collision with a car. It looked like the stay in hospital had given him a new freshness, a new lease of life. His real name was Robert. He got his nickname when we knocked for him one day and he came out eating a pear – no other reason, just that, pure and simple – and the name stuck ever since.

A few more of the lads came out of Horace's shed where they'd been having a fag, and a full-scale game developed when even more boys turned up. It eventually ended with a resounding win for the under-fourteens, 20–9. We packed up with the light fading and sat around for a while making plans for the weekend. Horace's voice could be heard yelling from his hut: 'Lock-up time, lads! Gates are closing! Everyone out!'

None of us took a blind bit of notice. It was nearly dark and Horace came across the grass wheeling his bike. 'Come on, boys,' he said, 'you'll get me the sack!'

'Oh, come on, Horace,' one of us said, 'just lock the gates. When we want to go home, we'll just climb over the fence. Who's to know we ain't climbed back in since you locked up and went home?'

Horace mumbled something about us lot getting him shot, then rode off on his bike and chained up the gates.

'Chelsea tomorrow, big Cup game! Anyone going?' I asked. 'Tony?'

'Count me in.'

'Jeff?'

'I'm there.'

No one else said a word

'Right then,' I said, 'three out of twenty-five ain't bad.'

A woman's voice interrupted our chat. 'Robert, Robert, are you in there, Robert?'

'Shit, it's me mum,' said Pear and he shot off into the darkness.

We all got up and headed towards the voice at the gate. Pear's mum saw me first. 'Martin, have you seen my Robert?'

'Yeah,' I said, 'he went with Horace when he locked up.'

'Right,' she said.

I could tell from her expression that she didn't believe me. She headed back in the direction of Pear's house.

We climbed over the locked gates and the gang split in different directions. 'See ya tomorrow,' said someone.

'Yeah, see ya,' we said and headed off down the alley towards home. 'Fancy Pear's mum coming looking for him! How embarrassing!' I laughed. 'Wait till I see him, I'm going to give him some shit!'

Jeff, Colin and Tony agreed that he hadn't heard the last of this. We would torment the life out of him.

Suddenly, a huge shape stepped out of the shadows and blocked our path. We all stopped in our tracks and shit ourselves. Who or what is this menacing figure? A rival fan out for revenge? A jealous boyfriend?

'There you are, you fucking little piece of shit!'

'Hello, Mum,' I gasped as the streetlight revealed her face. 'I'm just on my way home.'

'Well, let me help you on yer way!' she said, as she kicked me up the arse. 'What time do you call this!' she shouted as I ran up the road towards home. 'And don't run too fast, boy, because yer dad's waiting for you indoors with his belt and he's going to knock the living daylights out of ya!' She always said that when she was angry. I could hear the others laughing their bollocks off as I bombed home.

'Be gentle with him, Mrs King, he's the leader of the Chelsea Shed!' yelled Jeff to laughter from Tony and the others.

'Chelsea fucking Shed, I'll give him Chelsea fucking Shed! He won't sit down for a week, his arse will be that sore!'

The front door was open and the hallway light was on when I reached the house. I ran straight upstairs and took my clobber off as quickly as I could. I pulled the covers over my head and waited. Even the Chelsea players pinned up on my wall seemed to be looking down at me with expressions that said 'Looks like you're in big shit this time!'

The old girl came back and I heard her calling our cat in. 'Let's hope he's shit in the front room and then she'll leave me alone and take out her anger on him,' I thought. I peeped from under the covers and looked at the clock on my dressing table: 11.30 p.m., it says. 'Fucking hell, no wonder she's going apeshit,' I muttered.

I heard her come up the stairs. I was shitting myself, trembling with fear. Any minute now I was going to get it, a right good hiding. I knew as soon as she hit me I'd start crying. That way she'd leave me alone. The beating would be short and sweet.

I heard her walk along the passage and took a deep breath – but she didn't come into my room.

'I found him, Fred, up the fucking park with all them herberts he knocks about with,' she was saying to my dad.

'Yeah, all right, love,' the old man mumbled. By the sound of his voice he was half asleep already. 'I'll speak to him in the morning.'

The old girl rabbited on, almost talking to herself. There were no more replies from Dad – she must have sent him to sleep.

I tossed and turned but eventually fell asleep.

The alarm clock went and I heard Dad get up and go to the bathroom for a piss. I heard him filling up the kettle and putting it on the stove. The first fumes of the coal fire filtered up the stairs and then there was the sound of footsteps and the jangling of china as the old man carried up Mum's morning cup of tea. 'It's on the side, love,' I heard him say.

He pushed my bedroom door open. 'It's half six, boy,' he called.

I jumped up and got dressed, wiped a semi-damp flannel over my face, brushed my teeth and headed downstairs to face the music.

'Morning, Dad,' I said.

The old man was sitting with his back to me, staring into the roaring fire. He answered without looking round. 'Morning, boy. Wrap yourself up on that paper round of yours.'

I nodded.

Dad's head turned towards me: 'In late last night, weren't ya?'

'Yeah, I suppose I was a bit,' I agreed, 'I didn't realise it was so late.'

'You know your mother worries about ya, don't ya, boy?'

I nodded again.

Dad stoked up the fire and stuck two pieces of sliced bread on to the iron poker and proceeded to toast them above the hot coals. 'All mothers worry about their sons,' he said. 'My mum worried about me. She worried about me right up to the day your mother and I got married. Let her know where you are, boy, and you won't get in any trouble.'

'Okay,' I said, 'point taken.' I'd got off lightly there. 'Cheers, Dad,' I said.

He ruffled my hair and he handed me a slice of well-done toast. 'Butter that and get it down ya, boy.'

Funny bloke, the old man. He'd fly off the handle and lose his rag at the silliest things, and yet other times, when I thought I was going to get the shit knocked out of me, he was nice and calm and mellow. I could never work him out.

'Going to football today?' he asked, chewing on his breakfast.

'Yeah,' I said, as I put my coat on to go and do my paper round. 'It's Chelsea versus Norwich today, but I'm going to Tooting before the game. And, out of my paper-round money, I'm going to treat myself to a Ben Sherman and a sleeveless jumper I've seen in the shop at the Broadway.'

'Boy, do us a favour. When you go out, don't slam the front door. It shakes the whole house and it starts your mum off, and then I get it in the ear!'

'Righto, Pa,' I said, 'I'll see ya later.'

I opened the front door and pondered for a second what the old man had just said about the noise upsetting my mum. I opened the door quietly and even wider than necessary then put two hands on the doorknocker and slammed it as hard as I could. The glass nearly shattered with the force and rattled against the wood beading that held it in place. The frame and the door moved as one.

I was off up the garden path as fast as my legs would carry me. When I reached the gate, I looked back. The curtains in Mum's bedroom were pulled back and her face appeared at the window. You didn't have to be an expert in lip-reading to understand as she mouthed the words 'You fucking little git! Wait till I get my hands on you!'

I finished my paper round and went into Tooting on the bus. Half an hour later I was homeward bound with my new Ben Sherman shirt and a navy-blue sleeveless jumper. Every couple of minutes I was checking inside my plastic bag, making sure I hadn't lost my purchases and admiring my new clothes. When I got home everyone was out, so I slipped on my new shirt and jumper. I checked myself in the mirror from every possible angle. 'That'll do nicely,' I said to myself. No need for a coat, even though it was cold outside. It would give everyone the chance to admire my new gear.

I met up with Jeff and Tony and we took the tube from Wimbledon to Fulham Broadway. The train was packed with Chelsea fans heading for Stamford Bridge. The big Cup games down at the Bridge were always something special. There was always that air of expectancy – this could be the year when our team wins the Cup! Cup games had a different feel about them compared with the ordinary league matches.

The train pulled in at Fulham Broadway and there was the usual dash off the train and up the stairs and out onto the Fulham Road. We caught our breath and crossed the road to stand outside the White Hart pub opposite the station. There were still two hours to kick-off and already there were thousands of fans milling about. The café and the fish-and-chip shop were doing a roaring trade with queues a mile long.

Quite a few Norwich fans with their green-and-yellow scarves were walking about, mixing with the Chelsea fans, but no one took any notice of them. They waved their homemade banners above their heads. They were not there for any trouble but just to have a day out in London and make the most of seeing their team playing against a bigger club.

We walked down towards the North stand, which was the first entrance to the stadium. Thousands of Norwich fans were trying to get in through the turnstiles. Coppers on horseback tried to ease the crush on those queuing at the front. It looked like every Norwich fan was decked out in yellow-and-green scarves. Some had on three-foot-tall homemade top-hats with huge Norwich rosettes pinned on the front.

We headed down towards the Shed entrance. It was so packed that people were queuing out onto the Fulham Road.

'Let's try the Bovril entrance,' suggested Jeff. But it was the same there, with fans spewing out onto the road.

We stopped and looked at one another. 'There's only one thing for it,' I said. 'Let's go into the North stand with the Norwich fans. Loads of Chelsea boys will be doing the same.'

So that was it. We queued for the North stand along with thousands of Chelsea and Norwich fans. There were no police trying to segregate the fans, it was a 'let's just get everyone in the ground' policy.

After about half an hour of having the life nearly squeezed out of me, we were through the turnstiles and could breathe normally again. I checked I still had all my arms and legs and felt inside my pockets to make sure I hadn't lost any money.

It was a frightening experience trying to get into a big game.

You'd push and shove and, being below shoulder height of most people, you couldn't see what was going on. God forbid if someone were to fall over.

Anyway, we were in at last and we made our way along the back of the terraces and stood underneath the stand that looked like it was resting on stilts. It never looked safe to me – probably why I never sat there. 'Should be condemned,' I thought.

The Norwich fans packed under the stand came to life and chanted their team's name. It sounded loud as it echoed round the stand. The Chelsea fans in the Shed responded with a chant of 'Chelsea!' followed by 'You'll never take the Shed!' The Norwich fans jeered and a few gave the wankers sign back.

I turned to a Norwich fan standing right next to me. He was dressed like he could have been featured in *Farmers' Weekly*, with a chunky green-and-yellow scarf wrapped around his neck three or four times, with a knitted bobble-hat to match. All the Norwich lot were dressed the same. There were no skinheads amongst them. Their fans looked like they were waiting to be auditioned as extras for the cowboy telly show, *Rawhide*.

'Why were you jeering the Chelsea boys when they sang "You'll never take the Shed"?' I said to this fella.

He looked at his mate for the answer. He shrugged his shoulders and looked down. 'We ain't here for no trouble, mate, honest.'

'It's all right,' I said, 'we ain't looking for none.'

'Don't spoil their day out,' said Jeff, 'leave them alone!'

I started talking to these blokes. They were about my age and told me they'd come down to London for the game with their parents who'd let them go to the game on their own so long as they met up with them outside the stadium straight after the final whistle. One of them told me that Norwich didn't really have a mob of skinheads and that the only trouble he'd ever seen at a game was when Norwich played their local rivals, Ipswich. Then, he said, the whole town turned out for the ruck.

One interesting story he told me was about a group of Norwich fans that were fishermen. They often turned up at games dressed in their yellow oilskins. Apparently, after one game, they caught some away supporters tinkering with their boats. They gave chase and apprehended the culprits by tangling them up in their nets, which they'd tossed into the air. Every now and then these trawlermen could be seen in and around Carrow Road. Rumour had it that they mostly turned up at games on cold foggy nights when it was impossible to go out in their boats to fish.

The bloke laughed when I told him to fuck off.

'Trawlermen in fucking oilskins, catching rival fans in nets! Do you think I'm fucking stupid? Born yesterday? Come over on a banana boat? What sort of idiot would believe a daft story like that!'

In the end we had a good laugh with these two lads. Although they lived just a five-hour drive from us, they might as well have come from another planet. They couldn't believe there was trouble at nearly every Chelsea game. The whole skinhead culture was hard for them to take on board. The clothes, the music – they'd never even heard any reggae records or the Trojan label. They said it was because there weren't many 'darkies' (their word, not mine) living in Norfolk. Once a month they held a dance in the village hall and they played mostly '60s-type music – Elvis, Lonnie Donegan, The Beatles. 'But next week I'm going to turn up with my hair cropped and ask for some bluebeat sounds!' one of them said.

'You go for it, boy,' I laughed. 'Spread the word of the gospel according to all true skinheads!'

We shook hands and wished each other well. It had turned out to be a great afternoon.

There was no trouble at all that day and after the game the Norwich and Chelsea fans walked back to Fulham Broadway chatting happily. I even heard a couple of our boys arranging to meet some Norwich blokes up at the Norfolk Broads next summer.

Back at school on Monday morning, we all gathered together to exchange our football stories. West Ham had taken a huge mob up north. Spurs wrecked trains, again. Palace got run at home by some poxy little team. The Man United fans had nothing to report. Their game wasn't on telly. Chelsea and Norwich fans exchanged pleasantries. Quite a boring weekend, it seemed, but I'd other things on my mind.

Monday morning soon became Friday morning and before going to school I had a bath. Mum couldn't believe it. 'Fuck me, boy, have I forgot your birthday?' she cried.

'No, it's ice-skating today.'

'So what's the bath in aid of?' she queried.

'Nothing,' I said, splashing plenty of Brut all over me before rushing off to catch the bus.

I was the first one at school that day and I kicked a football up against the classroom wall while I waited for everyone else to turn up. Normally I'd go on the bus with Steve Ballard but I was in such a rush that morning with my princess on my mind that I totally forgot about him.

It wasn't long before the playground was full and a football match was in progress. After assembly I had Maths, then French. I daydreamed my way through Maths but paid some attention to French on account of the fact that the teacher wasn't a bad sort. Lovely arse and a nice firm pair of tits. 'I'd come me lot in about five seconds,' I thought. My dream was that she keeps me behind for detention one afternoon and we end up with me stripping her off in the book cupboard. I give her the seeing-to of her life. She tells me in that wonderful French accent of hers that I'm the best lover she's ever had. I light up a cigarette and we lie in each other's arms as she tells me how much she loves me. Dopey mare – can't she see she's only one of many women in my life, and that I'm only using her for my own devious ends?

French over, my mind switched to meeting the other girl of my dreams down at the ice-rink. When I get there, do I play hard to get and ignore her, let her chase me, that sort of thing, I wondered. Or should I go in straight away and get her behind the DJ's stand, rip her drawers off and shag her? Whatever I did it wouldn't involve spending any money on her, I thought, as I felt the last ten pence in my pocket.

I noticed the coach wasn't there yet. Normally it parked outside the school gates. It must be late.

After the break we made our way to the gym and from there the teacher usually led us down to the coach. But today when we got to the gym I noticed the five-a-side football nets had been set up.

'Right!' shouted the teacher. 'Boys get changed into their PE kits for indoor football. Girls get changed and it's netball with Mrs Smith outside. Chop chop! Let's see some action!' he finished, clapping his hands together loudly.

'Sir,' I said, 'I think you'll find our class goes ice-skating on Fridays.'

'Not any more, King, lad!' he said with a snide grin. 'The Council have run out of funds for outdoor activities, so it's back to football or cross-country running!'

I was gutted. The wind was taken out of my sails. How cruel was life! I was on the verge of meeting a right dollybird, maybe even getting engaged, and the Council run out of fucking money! I couldn't believe it, the girl of my dreams gone forever. I'd even had a bath! 'Better not waste my current cleanliness,' I thought. 'I'll be out on the pull tonight.'

Some you win, some you lose, bit like football really!

SEVEN

Marching On Together – Leeds United

'Careful, careful,' I said to Tony, 'don't overload the pram. If we break it the old girl will kill me. She uses it to collect firewood from the furniture-maker's – well, *she* don't, I do. She sends me round to the factory when they throw out all the off-cuts of wood, and uses them to get the coal fire going in the mornings.'

Today we were using the pram for another purpose. We were loading it up with lead and taking it down to the scrapyard. We had a good six pram-loads, if not more. A couple of younger kids who played football with us at the park tipped us off about a large consignment of lead which had been stripped from a disused factory roof by a couple of well-known local thieves who had the brains of rocking-horses. They'd been up on the roof and stripped it clean, but instead of taking it straight to the scrapyard, they decided to put it up until they could borrow their older brother's van. They were too well known by the local Old Bill to go wandering round the streets pushing pram-loads of lead. Tony and I, being up-and-coming entrepreneurs, decided to bunk off school and cash in on our new-found treasure-trove. Why risk your neck climbing around on roofs thirty foot off the ground when you could nick what had already been nicked, so to speak.

We carefully negotiated the bricks and broken concrete that lay strewn across the cracked roadway. The path led down to two huge metal gates where a sign saying 'Do Not Enter, Guard Dogs on Patrol' hung from the rusty wire mesh. Someone had made a hole in the mesh that was just big enough to wheel a pram through. Ours was so heavy it took the pair of us all our strength just to push it along. Every now and then we stopped for a breather and to wipe the sweat from our brows. At every corner we checked there were no policemen about. It was a two-mile trek from the disused factory to the scrap-yard, but eventually we got there. We unloaded the lead onto the weighing machine and the scrap man smiled as he told me to take my foot off the scales.

'Nice try, son,' he said. 'Three and half hundredweight there, boys,' and off he went into his office. He came back clutching four crumpled one-pound notes. 'There ya go, fellas, good to do business with ya.'

Tony and I were all smiles. 'Fucking hell, Tone, four quid!' I said as we walked away. 'And it's only the first lot!' I handed him two of the notes but he didn't look too happy. 'What's up?' I asked.

'I reckon he's stitched us up,' said Tony. 'If my dad or your dad took that lot in I bet they'd come out with more than four quid – probably double that. He thinks we're young and silly, so he's fucked us up!'

'Yeah,' I said, 'and we've fucked someone else up by pinching their lead! It's called swings and roundabouts, Tone.'

On the way back to the factory for the next batch we stopped at Frank's Café and ordered sausage, egg, chips and beans twice. While Frank was busy cooking in the kitchen, we got on the five-in-a-line pinball machine. If you got three balls in a line, you won a pound; four in a line won you three pounds; and five in a line a fiver. We were experts on the machines simply because we were always playing them. It was easy money, and on the first game we won a pound each.

'Grub's up!' shouted Frank, and we got stuck in to the food.

'Hungry work, this scrap-metal game,' said Tony.

'Better than going to school,' I replied, stuffing another sausage in my mouth.

'Talking of school,' interrupted Frank, 'why aren't you two there?'

'I've got a note from me mum saying that I can have the day off,' I said.

'What, so you can go pinching lead?' asked Frank.

'How do you know we've been nicking lead?' I gasped.

'By the colour of your hands. And your faces are rotten – it looks like you've been helping the coalman,' Frank laughed.

We wiped the empty plates with the last of the bread and butter and said goodbye to Frank. Mum's pram was still parked outside – no one had pinched it – so we were still in business. Five minutes later we squeezed back through the factory gates and began to fill the pram with more lead. This time we stacked it up even higher and the front wheels began to buckle and creak outwards with the weight. We both gave it a good hard push and slowly the wheels started to turn. The first kerb we came to was difficult and we had heave and pull to get it up onto the footpath. And from then on we followed the same route as the first journey. We reached the scrapyard with sweat pouring down our faces.

The scrap man sauntered out of his office and flicked his dog-end to the ground. 'Well, well,' he said, 'if it isn't the Black and White Minstrels back with another load.'

'Who's the Black and White Minstrels?' asked Tony.

I tried to explain. 'It's that show on a Saturday night on the telly, where white people dress up in white suits and white gloves, black up their faces and sing "Mammy" and shit like that.' Tony looked blank. 'Well, it's for older people, anyway,' I said, 'the sort of show your mum and dad or your nan would watch.'

He was still none the wiser as we loaded the lead onto the scales. White people blacking up their faces, making out they're black, I could see him thinking. Are they fucking mad?

'That's four and half hundredweight,' said the scrap man, checking where my feet were positioned. He was watching us like hawks this time and I could tell he didn't trust us. He walked off to get us some money.

'Me dad said that wasn't a very good price you gave us for the last lot!' I called after him.

'What, your dad in the scrap game, is he?' asked the man as he came back.

'No, but he knows the prices,' I said as he handed over some cash.

'Go on, fuck off out of it, you cheeky little gits.'

We pushed the pram out onto the road clutching five one-pound notes and some coins.

'What a result!' I said. 'That's over nine pounds we've had for just a couple of hours' work. We should go into the scrap game when we leave school, Tone – be a good earner.'

'I bet my old man doesn't earn that in a week,' said Tony.

We passed Frank's Café. He was sitting on the front step having a cup of tea and a fag. 'More pinball, lads?' he called. 'How about some tea or coffee?'

'No thanks, Frank,' I said, 'we've got work to do.'

Frank shook his head and laughed.

'I bet there's another three pram-loads,' said Tony as we hurried back towards our nest-egg. We stopped at the corner shop at the top of my street to buy a can of Coke each. The woman behind the counter looked at us strangely, staring at our black faces. She should have known me – I'd done a paper round there for the last three years.

'Well, another three pram-loads adds up to another fifteen quid,' said Tony. We rubbed our hands together at the prospect of being rich.

We climbed back through the hole in the gate and looked at one another in horror as we saw that the rest of the lead had disappeared.

'Fucking thieving bastards!' we gasped at the same time.

'What's happened to honour amongst thieves?' said Tony.

Then we heard someone shouting. 'Oi, you two, stay where you are!' Coming towards us were two big burly men. 'Don't move!' they yelled.

Bollocks to them! Tony and I were off. It was a good two hundred yards to the hole in the gate and the pram was slowing us down. The men were getting closer and closer. They were still shouting but I could no longer make out what they were saying. The nearer they got the bigger they looked. Fuck this for a game of soldiers!

'Ditch the pram!' panted Tony.

'Fuck off!' I yelled, gulping in some air. 'The old girl will kill me if I lose her pram!'

Tony reached the gate first and pulled back the wire to let me through. The men were just twenty yards away and closing. We sprinted across the road and ducked down an alleyway, but I looked back and saw they were still chasing us. We tore down the alley, scattering metal dustbins behind us. I'd seen James Bond do that once in a film to slow his pursuers down. The noise of the clattering lids set off all the local dogs barking.

We came out onto a main road. On the other side was another alley. We dodged the traffic as we crossed the road and carried on. The men were still on our case, but we'd put a bit of distance between us now.

Tony suddenly stopped and I nearly ran into the back of him as he bent over trying to catch his breath. He wasn't looking too clever, and his face was bright red. 'I can't run any more,' he gasped. 'I've got a stitch.'

I glanced over my shoulder and saw the men had made up some ground. I could see the look of anger on their faces. 'Quick! Get in the pram!' I commanded.

'No, leave me,' he wheezed. 'I won't grass you up.'

'Fuck off,' I said, and rammed the pram into the back of his legs. He fell backwards into it and we took off with Tony lying back in the pram. We dashed across streets and in and out of alleys until we lost the two men.

We headed for the park where we hid the pram behind Horace's shed and nipped inside to have a chat with him and catch our breath.

'Good God!' said Horace, looking at us. 'What the Dickens have you two been up to?'

We checked ourselves in Horace's little cracked mirror. Black dust from the lead and sweat had mixed together and run down our faces giving them a zebra-striped effect.

'Your mothers will go mad when they see you,' said Horace. 'You two had better clean yourselves up, but have a cup of tea first.'

That was Horace all over – tea first, then tackle any problems. He was a kind man with a good heart.

As Horace filled up the kettle and laid out the teacups, Tony and I had time to wonder who the two blokes were who'd chased us.

'Old Bill, I reckon,' said Tony.

'No!' I shook my head. 'Builders, I reckon. They were definitely builders or demolition men, and they've come on the site, seen all the lead missing, seen us with the getaway pram, and we're prime suspects.'

Horace handed us our tea and opened some custard creams. 'I know it's none of my business, boys, but are you two in trouble? Because if you are, the first thing you should do is get all that muck off your faces and get that pram back home. I can tell just by looking at you that you've been up to no good.'

'Point taken,' I said to Horace. 'Come on, Tone,' I said as we finished our tea, 'thanks a lot, Horace, catch ya later.'

'Where are we going?' asked Tony

'To get rid of this pram,' I told him. 'It's a piece of incriminating evidence.'

We left the park and headed for my house. At the top of my road, I nipped into a phone box and called home. There was no answer. I hung up. 'Right, the old girl's over her sister's in Streatham, or she's gone to the bingo.' I found the key for the front door underneath a flowerpot in the front porch and let myself in, wheeling the pram through and putting it in the back shed.

Tony followed me. 'Won't your mum have noticed it's been missing?' he asked.

'Well, she ain't noticed it missing for the last five years on Bonfire Night when I've been out doing "Penny for the Guy", so I don't suppose she's missed it today,' I replied.

I shut the shed door and I told Tony to wait there. I ran upstairs and come down with two pairs of swimming trunks and a couple of towels. I handed a set to Tony. He looked at me, puzzled.

'Come on,' I said, 'let's go to Mitcham swimming-baths to get cleaned up.'

'You're joking,' saidTony.

'Well, you come up with a better suggestion.We can't get cleaned up here. If the old girl comes home and finds us in the bathroom together she'll think we're a couple of bum bandits. Plus she's going to ask questions about why we look like Desmond Dekker, so come on, let's go.'

At the swimming-baths the woman behind the counter gave us a suspicious look. 'Here we go again,' I thought, 'more aggro.'

'You ain't the two who was in here the other week that got thrown out for weeing into the pool from the public gallery?' she demanded.

We both tried not to laugh.

'Because if you are,' she went on, 'I regret to inform you that you have both been barred indefinitely.'

'No, sorry,' I said, 'you've got the wrong people.'

'Okay,' she said, 'in you go.'

Mitcham swimming-baths was a bit of a dodge city in the world of swimming-pools. It was lawless: kids would be diving off the balcony in the public gallery, while others on the top diving board would piss on the swimmers below. Lockers were broken into and vending-machines ransacked. It was a real war zone.Anyway, we were only in there to have a swim and wash off our hard day's work.The chemicals in the water soon had our hands and faces and the rest of us clean.

Afterwards, we met some kids from our school getting off the bus on their way home. 'Where've you two been?' asked a few of our schoolmates.

'Earning a living,' I replied.

Tony and I went back to my house and Mum was just back from the bingo. 'All right, boy, how was school?' she asked.

'Yeah, fine,' I replied.

'Had swimming today, then?' she said, noticing the towel under my arm.

'Yeah, yeah,' I replied. There wasn't much that got past the old girl.

Tony and I went upstairs and laid what money we had left out on my bed.

'You know what, Kingy,' he said, counting his money, 'we've got enough to go up to Leeds this Saturday to watch Chelsea play.'

'Yeah!' I said. 'I'll hold all the money and hide it in my wardrobe until we go to football.'

I tucked the cash inside my Harrington jacket and we agreed we wouldn't break into it until our journey up north. By the look of it we'd pulled off quite a coup.

'Let's go over the park,' suggested Tony, 'and see if anyone's heard anything about our mission.'

But no one had heard anything. It was the same at school the next day. My letter from my mum explaining my absence the previous day, together with her forged signature, didn't even get a second glance from my teacher. No one in school mentioned our little piece of skulduggery.

On the Friday before the game at Leeds, I did my 'what a good boy' act. I ran a few errands for Mum, and when Dad came home from work I helped him water the back garden, even going as far as asking him names of certain plants. But when he went on a bit, telling me their Latin names, I had to turn away to yawn. Still, it did the trick and they said I could go to Leeds so long as I went with Jeff and Tony, promised to behave myself and could finance the trip.

As usual for a game up north, we arrived at King's Cross before anyone else. I'd done my paper round in record time, even throwing a stone up at Jeff's bedroom window on the way past to make sure he was awake. We had plenty of money on us, so we loaded up with all sorts of goodies from the shop at the station. Sweets, crisps, drinks, chewing-gum, magazines and comics – you name it, we bought it. Today we weren't going to get bored on the long journey.

It wasn't long before more Chelsea fans began to drift in to the station. Most were dressed in their dark Crombie overcoats which nearly met the Dr Marten boots which came halfway up their legs. A few of the main faces also turned up, and by the time everyone had bought their tickets, a two hundred-strong Chelsea mob was on the next train. About four hours later, we arrived at Leeds.

The journey up had been one of the quietest with any travelling Chelsea mob I could remember. Maybe it was the fear of the unknown – not many London teams went to Elland Road. They had a big following, home and away, and last season down at the Bridge a hundred or so Leeds fans had tried to take the Shed. If their numbers had been larger, and if the Old Bill hadn't intervened, I reckoned they would have succeeded.

The train stopped and we got off. Everyone was waiting for one of our lot to take the initiative and lead the mob. We stood around for a couple of minutes before someone said, 'Let's go!' We moved across the station and out onto the street. Joe Public stopped what they were doing and watched as this strange-looking group of young men filed out on to the streets of Leeds city centre. Across the other side of the road were a dozen or so youths, a few of whom had Leeds United scarves tied round their necks. They seemed a bit on edge.

'Don't run at them,' warned the boys at the front. 'Take it nice and easy, we don't want to get split up this early.'

Give that man a medal for common sense, I was thinking.

A few of our lot walked towards the Leeds boys, who took off down a side road. We didn't see their arses for dust.

'This way!' came a shout from the front. 'Keep it nice and tight.'

We came to a row of shops. There was a café there, and standing outside was a group of blokes in leather jackets. A couple of motor-bikes were parked at the kerb. 'Greasers!' someone shouted. The café emptied as about twenty bikers came out. A bloke at the front was waving a chair above his head, but before he can throw it at us, someone ran over from our side and cracked him one on the nose. He dropped the chair and covered his face with his hands. Blood trickled through his fingers and spots of it dripped onto the footpath. A Tizer bottle was hurled into the air. It smashed in amongst the Greasers. Their bikes were kicked over, the café window was put in and the sound of shattering glass sent the group in every direction. The chef came running out, ranting and raving in Greek or Italian, his grease-covered apron hanging from his waist. He waved his fists in the air and gestured that he was going to cut someone's throat.

'Fuck off, Dago!' I heard someone shout, and a bottle whistled past his head.

'Christa, Mama Donna!' he said and ran back inside.

The police arrived and, judging by their response, didn't seem too bothered about what was going on. The local tough boys had not been able to live up to their hard-nut image, and by the look of things the Old Bill found it quite funny that we'd done something they would probably have loved to have done ages ago.

'Come on, lads, keep moving, the ground's straight on,' said the copper at the front. A couple of policemen positioned themselves at the front of our mob and walked with us towards the stadium. A pub appeared on our right and some of our lot started to cross the road towards it. The few Leeds fans drinking outside didn't hang about and were inside like a shot. One or two faces appeared at the window and watched as we walked past.

I could feel this mob growing in confidence: three scrapes, no injuries, and now everyone's got the flavour. A few of the boys at the back started to shout to the main mob, 'Wait, wait!' and as we looked behind, the pub we had just passed had emptied out, the occupants deciding they quite fancied a ruck after all. The two coppers with us quickly got in front of the Leeds fans and pushed them back into the pub. The fans went back inside without too much fuss.

'Leeds, Leeds, Leeds!' they chanted, in a half-hearted attempt to get at us. If they'd really wanted a fight, they'd have been out of the pub before we even got there.

We came to a crossroads and saw Leeds fans milling about outside a chip shop. A few others were spread out, standing around talking. We got within twenty yards of them and the street cleared, the Leeds fans disappearing up little alleyways. The smell of fish and chips wafted into the air, but none of our lads stopped, no matter how hungry they were. Today it was more important to stick together, and not allow ourselves to be picked off by a Leeds mob. We'd done well so far.

By now we could see the floodlights of the ground, and there were more and more people hanging around. The Old Bill, watching from street corners, gave us the once-over, but didn't make a move. A few Leeds boys came out of a side street and walked towards us but a couple of coppers on horseback rode over and scattered them.

'Leeds up ahead!' someone shouted. We pushed our way to the front. The call didn't give us much notice as I was kicked up the arse by a forty-year-old Leeds fan right away.

'Fuck off back to London, you Cockney wanker!' he shouted, as pieces of the pie he'd been eating splattered over me.

'Fuck off, lard arse!' I retorted, 'Go on a diet, you fat dirty bastard!'

One of the boys spat at him and he backed off. None of his mates looked like they wanted to help him and he realised he was on his own. 'Officer, Officer!' said Fatty to the copper on horseback. 'That kid just spat at me!'

'Which one?' asked the policeman.

'The one with the cropped hair,' said Tubby.

'Well, that's anyone from two hundred of this lot,' said the copper as he rode off to divert more trouble up ahead. Fatso melted into the crowd as we regrouped, nice and tight.

A huge Leeds mob suddenly came from round the corner and ran straight into us, fists and boots flying. Fans on both sides were punched to the ground but managed to scramble back to their feet. We were backed up against the turnstiles and Leeds fans queuing to get in started joining in the attack. It was all getting a bit nasty and looked like our luck was running out.

'Leeds, Leeds, Leeds!' they chanted.

A Chelsea fan pulled what looked like a steel comb from his pocket and slashed a Leeds boy across the cheek. The lads around him backed off and this was the turning point. A gap opened up between the two mobs. When they saw the cut face and the blood, the Leeds fans knew the Chelsea mob meant business.

The Old Bill came in with their dogs and forced us one way and the Leeds firm the other. The St John's Ambulance men laid the bloke with the cut face down onto the footpath while a copper screamed into his radio for help. I bet that guy hated Chelsea for the rest of his life. He would never be able to forget what happened. Every time he looked in a mirror he'd think of our lot. Still, he must have been up for it, otherwise he wouldn't have been at the front of their mob.

The Old Bill forced us into the ground through the turnstiles. I didn't pay, just jumped over and mingled with the crowd. The Leeds fans outside were making one last charge at the fifty or so Chelsea boys left on the other side of the turnstiles. You could hear the ruck as a barrage of bricks and bottles hit the corrugated sheeting above the Chelsea fans' heads. More shouts of 'Leeds, Leeds, Leeds!' followed.

I found Tony and Jeff and wondered where the fuck we were.

'The Old Bill told me that they've put us in this end for our own safety,' said Jeff.

We made our way onto the terraces and discovered to everyone's surprise the police had only put us in the Leeds end. Hundreds of Leeds fans backed off as we all squeezed into the packed terrace of the Kop. We'd been well and truly set up, no doubt about that.

'Stick together, Chelsea!' said our main face as he pushed his way through the Leeds crowd. We followed and it was like the Red Sea parting. We stopped at the back and a few scuffles broke out, but we were more than holding our own. We'd done well and our mob was still together, although looking round I could see a few of our lot were sporting shiners and split lips. Jeff and Tony laughed when I showed them Fatso's footprint on the arse of my white Sta-prest.

I scanned the terraces for any blue and white, but it seemed we were the only Chelsea fans in the ground. The Old Bill arrived and formed a human shield around us. Word soon spread among the Leeds lads that we were in their end and every one of them who fancied himself as a rucker stood on the other side of the Old Bill and gave us abuse.

'Come on, you little wanker!' one of their big hairy-arsed beer monsters said to me. 'You and me outside!'

'He's brave,' I thought. 'There are bigger blokes than me with our lot, and this dipstick singles me out.'

Chelsea nearly scored and the Leeds mob pushed towards us from every direction. 'Leeds, Leeds, Leeds!' they chanted. The police did a marvellous job restraining these thugs – but wasn't it their idea to put us in here in the first place?

There were only ten minutes to go and I didn't hold out much hope of getting out of there alive. None of their lot was watching the game – all their eyes seemed to be on us. They turned their attention to a couple of girls who were with our mob and started giving all the usual old shit like 'Show us yer tits!' and 'Come over here with some real men'. Fair play to the girls, though: they gave as good as they got.

The game ended and the Leeds fans sang that we'd never make the station. To my surprise the Old Bill led us out with the Leeds fans. As we started heading down the huge concrete terrace a fight broke out but because we had the high ground, we seemed to be getting the upper hand.

I spotted a Chelsea fan waving a hammer about. A Leeds fan tried to kick him and he caught the lad high on the temple with the hammer. The Leeds fan went down – he was spark out. The Chelsea fan handed the hammer to one of the girls, who quickly dropped it into the bag she had hanging from her shoulder. A few Leeds fans pointed out the attacker to a copper. The girl walked away and blended into the crowd.

'He's just done our mate with a hammer!' the Leeds mob told the policeman, who promptly stopped and searched the Chelsea fan. Of course he found nothing.

'Piss off,' said the copper and pushed the Leeds fans down the terraces.

We came out onto the street and I couldn't believe the size of the crowd waiting for us. We'd have to fight our way out of the ground. I knew if we showed any fear, that Leeds mob would kill us. They charged into us from the front, and as we struck back I'd never been so scared in my life.

'Watch yer back,' someone shouted as they came at us from behind. The police horses moved in and we took the chance to get across to the other side of the road. The Leeds crowd backed off for a moment, just long enough for us to all get together. There was a lull in the action and we moved off. The Old Bill positioned themselves between us and the Leeds mob.

Leeds started to charge from the side and we turned to face them. It was toe to toe in the street. Another Leeds mob came at us from the rear. Behind was a carpark which we backed off into, and the Old Bill stopped the Leeds mob from coming any closer. There was an exit at the other side and we all headed for that. The wall round the carpark was the only reason we were still alive – that and the Old Bill. We were well outnumbered and should by rights be mincemeat, but we knew that if we didn't see this through and stick together we were finished, big time.

'Stick together!' barked one of our main men. 'Let's get into the street up in front of us and reorganise.'

But there was no time for that as a Leeds mob came round the corner and walked towards us. The ones at the front were armed with bricks and bottles. When they got to within twenty feet of us they let fly with all their ammo. We just carried on towards them and they were on their toes. They stopped at a street corner and tried to regroup but we had no intention of letting them come at us again. We ran towards them at top speed. We were doing a lot better now that there was more room to manoeuvre and we could see what was coming at us and from where.

'They'll be back,' said one of our boys.

There was a bus-stop up ahead and any Leeds fans waiting for their bus soon disappeared. The Leeds mob appeared out of a side street and this time there were over a hundred of them. Again, they lobbed anything they could lay their hands on at us. We turned to face them and they started to retreat. They were walking backwards slowly, telling each other to stand still, but carrying on moving backwards.

A few of our lads caught them up and were in amongst them. Blows were exchanged and a few more of us ran in to add a bit of extra weight. The Leeds lot started to turn and run and then suddenly they stopped and turned back to face us. Out of an alleyway was pouring a steady stream of reinforcements. They were well up for it now. They walked towards us and we all looked at each other. If any-one ran now, we'd be done for. It was at times like this that your mob had to stick together. I could see what was on everyone's mind: 'We've done well all day – let's not spoil it now.'

The right people were up in the front line, and they took the initiative. 'Walk, Chelsea!' the boss man shouted. 'Walk!' And we walked towards the Leeds firm at funeral-procession speed. The Leeds mob halted. 'Yes!' went up the shout and we ran at them. A few of their boys stood and threw a couple of half-hearted punches and kicks, but the majority fled. Some jumped over garden walls, look-ing for a safe haven. Others dived under parked cars, fucking cowards.

Their main lot ran into a block of flats and the rest disappeared up the alley they'd just come from. We decided not to follow them onto the estate and instead turned and went back out onto the main road towards the railway station, where we all knew it would be Leeds' last chance to make a show. They knew we'd done well today.

A few coppers showed up with dogs and followed us along the road. Someone noticed that a mob of around fifty Leeds fans were following us at a safe distance. On every side street we passed, their boys were spotted monitoring our progress.

The station came into view up ahead and there were Old Bill everywhere. We saw some activity to our right and by the look of it the police were struggling to control a huge Leeds mob.

For a moment it felt like the dam would burst and the raging Leeds fans would pour out our way, but the Old Bill were making sure they didn't get anywhere near us. The dogs were going berserk, straining at the leash. One chomp, that's all they wanted, just one bite and taste of human flesh.

'Leeds, Leeds, Leeds!' the fans chanted, knowing that if they couldn't punch our heads in, maybe this monotonous chant would surely do our heads in instead.

We went into the station and, as usual at away games, the train was waiting to take us back to London. If only trains were this punctual in everyday life. It wasn't too long before the train pulled out and we were on our way. The mood on board was jubilant and the whole mob knew we'd done exceptionally well that day, and that every single person had played their part. I think we shocked the Leeds fans first of all by turning up and then by giving a good account of ourselves. Leeds at Elland Road were a force to be reckoned with, no doubt about that.

To our surprise the train had a buffet car. There hadn't been one on the journey up – perhaps they'd laid one on for us since we'd given such a good performance. We bought the works: tea, Coke, pasties, sandwiches, pies, crisps and sweets. The only problem was we'd lost our seats. Some knackered Chelsea boys were sprawled out on them trying to get some kip. We walked along the train with our stash, but couldn't find anywhere we could sit down and tuck in. We came to the first-class compartments and slid the door open and just flopped down. We pulled our boots off to give our tired feet a chance to get some air. We took our coats off and pulled our braces down to our waists.

'How much do I owe you for my grub?' Jeff asked me.

'Nothing,' I said. 'It's on me and Tony.'

Jeff look puzzled. 'No, don't fuck about,' he said.

'Jeff, it's on us!' I said.

'Okay, okay,' he said, and balanced a pork pie, a packet of crisps and a Coke all in one hand.

The door slid open and in walked the guard. 'Tickets, please,' he said with a smirk, no doubt thinking, 'I know these little fuckers ain't got first-class tickets.'

We showed him our tickets.

'Sorry, lads, these are not first-class tickets, so I suggest you gather all your stuff together and go back down the train to where your tickets are valid. Or you can pay another three pounds and stay where you are, but I suppose you being schoolkids, three pounds is a lot of money.'

I still had six pounds left from our lead money. I pulled it from my pocket and peeled off three one-pound notes. 'There you go, mate,' I said to the shocked guard, and he handed me three first-class tickets. 'Bet you don't earn that in a week!'

'Cheeky bastard!' he mumbled under his breath.

Jeff was now totally bemused. 'What the fuck have you two little bastards been up to?'

I laughed. 'Shall I tell him, Tone, or will you?'

There's no answer from Tony. The day's events had caught up with him and he was fast asleep.

'Well, the other day me and Tony found some –' But before I could finish, Jeff was asleep as well. Fucking good company, these two.

A day up at Leeds, all the food you could eat, first-class travel. I must have been dreaming.

EIGHT

London Overspill

'I can remember standing in the station in this exact spot about three or four years ago, Kingy,' said Jeff. 'You had on a woollen blue-and-white scarf your nan had knitted you, if I remember rightly!'

I nodded in agreement, slightly embarrassed.

'We were off to Spurs, me, you and Tony.'

'Yes, yes, your memory hasn't failed you,' I said. 'Now shut up!'

Jeff was right. I'd gone with him to Spurs a few years ago. That was the day I'd got my first experience of aggro at football and I'd been hooked on the whole scene ever since: the travelling to the game with mates, meeting new faces, becoming one of the chaps, the main faces nodding in my direction or even saying hello, the clothes and seeing what was in fashion (and, more importantly, seeing what was not), the game itself, the punch-ups – the whole thing had become a way of life. I'd even pissed off my girlfriend, Lynda, because I'd chosen to go to the match with my mates rather than go shopping with her to Croydon. Football won over shopping every time.

I'd been going out with Lynda for about six months now, and she saw Saturday as the day we should spend together, when I should take her shopping, go arm in arm round all the shops, maybe have a Wimpy, visit her nan, take her little brother out to the park and sail his model boat on the lake. Bollocks to that! Saturday was for football, and I wasn't giving that up for no one, not even in exchange for a regular bit of fanny. I didn't mind going out on Saturdays with her during the summer because the football season was over, but whatever way you looked at it, today the boys and I were going up to Ipswich to see Chelsea play at Portman Road.

As usual, we arrived at Liverpool Street Station far too early. It only took about an hour and a half to get to Ipswich and we were going for the nine o'clock train, meaning we'd be up there by about ten thirty. There were a few Chelsea fans milling about, but I'd not heard of any big meets being arranged or that there was any specific train all our mob were to catch. It was probably because Ipswich weren't renowned for having a big firm that were up for a row. It seemed all the London clubs went in the Ipswich end and cleared it, so I supposed our lot would meet up in or around the ground. At every away game I'd been to this season we'd gone in the home team's end. We even tried to get into the Spion Kop at Anfield but were turned away by the Old Bill. I don't know how long we would have lasted in there.

A few of the West Ham boys from school had gone to Ipswich for an evening kick-off and although they hadn't taken a big mob up there, the lads who went cleared the Ipswich end within seconds of getting inside the ground.

'We only sang "West Ham" once,' my mate said, 'and we cleared their end. The Ipswich boys were onto the pitch in seconds.'

It sounded like they weren't very game. Only a handful of Chelsea fans were on our train, so the plan was that when we reached Ipswich, we'd hang out in a café until we bumped into a few familiar faces.

It was a fairly warm day, so Tony and I were wearing our Harrington jackets with just a Fred Perry underneath. For some reason Jeff had on a Crombie overcoat. It soon became clear why. He took a can of light ale from his inside pocket and tore off the ring pull. 'Want one, Kingy?' he said, as he took another one from his coat.

'No thanks,' I replied. If the truth be told, I couldn't stand the taste or smell of beer. I'd pinched a can of Watney's Pale Ale from my dad's drinks cabinet once and was horrified by the taste. It was disgusting. I'd been at family parties and seen adults knocking this stuff back, and the way they acted after a few drinks made me curious to see what it tasted like. It definitely wasn't for me. Give me a cream soda or a Tizer any day.

Tony took a can from Jeff and the pair of them gulped the beer down and then moved on to another couple.

'Sure you don't want one, Kingy?' asked Jeff, opening his third.

We arrived at Ipswich with Jeff and Tony half pissed. The station reminded me of something out of an Enid Blyton story with its flower boxes and tubs of plants all along the platform. I could imagine the Famous Five coming to Ipswich for their summer hols and finding smugglers and buried treasure. It was not the sort of place for a punch-up at football.

We left the station and asked a couple of local old codgers where we might find a café or coffee shop. They gave us a blank look.

'I know you might find our accents a bit strange,' I said. 'That's because we're from Russia.' My humour, or lack of it, made no impression.

Jeff took over. 'Excuse me, ladies, can you point us in the direction of any caff or coffee shop, somewhere your good selves would find appropriate and feel at home?'

'Oh, right,' said one of the old girls.

'See, Kingy,' said Jeff, 'leave it to me. Just a little bit of patience and charm goes a long way.'

The old dollies smiled and began to give us directions. 'Go straight down to the end of this road, turn left, then right, straight on for about a mile then you come to a roundabout. Go straight across that and then carry on for about two miles.'

'Hang on, love,' Jeff interrupted. 'By sending us all that way, aren't we heading out of town?'

'Well, I'm sending you towards the countryside, because you won't find any cows in the town centre,' said the old girl.

'What cows?' asked Jeff. 'We ain't looking for no cows.'

'Hang on a minute,' said the woman. 'You just asked me where you could find a calf and isn't a calf a young cow?'

I don't know which one of us doubled up with laughter first, but in the end we were all crying with laughter, tears streaming down our faces. I even got a stitch in my stomach.

'Fucking dopey mare!' I said, wiping tears from my eyes.

'Fucking cows,' gasped Jeff, still bent double.

'Well, you're looking for a calf,' said Tony, impersonating the old girl's accent.

The two women toddled off, still wondering why we collapsed in fits of laughter.

After a few minutes we pulled ourselves together and decided to have a walk around the town. There was no sign of any football fans. There was hardly sign of any life at all, come to that. The folk in this sleepy Suffolk town didn't get up and out very early by the look of it. Perhaps, on second thoughts, the Famous Five would give this place a miss.

Eventually we found a café. Jeff was straight onto the pinball and Tony and I ordered up the breakfast. The smell of eggs and bacon cooking made us feel hungry. Jeff joined us as we scoffed the breakfast down in no time at all. It was a lovely bit of grub. Tony nudged me as three girls aged about sixteen came in. They looked over and one whispered something to the other two and all three giggled.

'Hello, girls, care to join us?' called Tony as I put our empty plates on the next table. I grabbed another couple of chairs and wiped the table down with my hand. I didn't want them thinking we were a bunch of scruffy bastards.

'Plenty of room, come and join us,' I said.

The girls strolled over carrying their bottles of Coke with straws and plonked themselves down. They all started giggling again and went red. 'Hello,' said one of them. She had bright blue eyeshadow and black roots showing through her dyed blonde hair. 'You boys here for the football?'

'No, we're here working on a building site,' I said. 'We're brick-layers, come up from London.'

The girl smiled.

'We're on a big contract over near the football ground.'

'Oh yeah,' said her mate with the frizzy perm and wonky nose as she chewed nervously on the straw hanging from her drink. 'Got any fags?' she asked.

'Sorry, love, I can't afford to smoke.' As soon as I said it I knew I'd dropped a bollock. *Fuck it, they know I'm lying. I've been sussed.*

'I thought you was a bricklayer,' said Blondie and everyone laughed.

'Well, I'm an apprentice bricklayer, that's what I meant,' I said, trying to dig myself out. 'I'm not really earning that much money, but Jeff and Tony are both fully fledged brickies, and even if they haven't got any fags, I'm sure they'd buy you a packet.' I looked at Jeff and Tony. *That'll teach you two wankers to laugh at me.*

'You from around these parts?' Tony asked the girls.

'Not originally,' said Blondie, 'Me and my sister Tracy' – she pointed at the straw-sucker – 'moved up here with my mum and dad from Dagenham about five years ago. My friend here, Julie' – pointing at her mate with the ginger hair cut in an afro like Jimi Hendrix – 'she's from Peckham in south-east London and she came here with her family at the same time as us. We moved in next door to one another on the same day and our two dads work together, and all of us go to the same school.'

'You've even got the same hairdresser by the looks of it,' I said.

Past the window filed a large group of Chelsea fans. We recognised a few of the faces. We finished up our drinks, pecked the girls on the cheek and told them how lovely they were. They looked like they were about to burst into tears.

'Time to go, boys,' said Jeff, and we hurried out of the café.

'Nice to meet you, girls!' I shouted as we caught the tail end of the mob.

We nodded to a few of the familiar faces and they nodded back. We headed off through the town centre and the locals stopped and stared at this strange group parading through the streets. A few of the Chelsea boys were stripped to the waist and trying to catch the eye of any young girl out doing her Saturday shopping. Apart from the three young birds in the café, though, the average age of the women we passed looked to be about sixty. 'Ipswich must be known as God's waiting-room,' I said to Tony. 'It's like Eastbourne without the sea.'

'I bet the discos are a bit lively,' he laughed.

We passed a bingo hall and hundreds of old people were queuing to get in. It must have been the highlight of their week. A few of our lot shouted comments at the queue and some of the old girls waved back. A man in a suit and dickie bow opened the doors and all the old grunters pushed forward.

'Hope you're going to behave yourselves, boys,' called one old dolly.

'Show us yer tits, love!' one of our mob shouted back.

'Maybe a few years ago,' came back the reply from the crowd of pensioners.

We arrived at the ground and the boys broke into a chant of 'Chelsea, Chelsea!' It was only an hour to kick-off but the place was almost deserted. Programme sellers, rosette sellers and hotdog vendors were shouting their wares but no one was buying.

'It don't look very lively,' said someone.

We walked around the ground. The Chelsea mob was getting bigger. Our crowd looked pissed off with the lack of action.

I spotted Eccles up the front. 'Stop here, lads,' he was saying. 'Let's get everyone together and then we're going into the ground.'

The mob had swollen to a good three or four hundred. We queued at the turnstiles and, once through, made our way out onto the terraces. The stadium was almost empty, apart from our end which was rapidly filling with Chelsea fans.

'That's the Ipswich end of the ground,' someone told us and pointed to where their boys normally stood. Today their spot was overrun with Chelsea fans.

We made our way down the terraces and stood directly behind the goal. The sun was shining and it was a lovely warm day, ideal for watching football. Most people sprawled out on the steps, bare-chested. The boys took the piss out of me. If a police dog got hold of me, they joked, it would bury me on the pitch, thinking I was a bone. Was I really that skinny?

Ten minutes before kick-off and the ground began to fill up. We couldn't work out why the Ipswich fans had arrived so late. 'Perhaps they've been to the bingo!' said Jeff.

The Chelsea team came out for a warm-up and got a rousing reception. The fans chanted each player's name in turn, and the player then waved to the crowd. Peter Osgood got the biggest cheer. The Chelsea crowd loved him. He was definitely the king of Stamford Bridge. They disappeared back down the tunnel and minutes later Ipswich came out led by their mascot.

'Is that a kid or a sixty-year-old midget?' I asked.

The Chelsea fans booed the Ipswich team loudly. Their goalkeeper ran towards our end and put his cap and gloves in the back of the net. He turned and took some practice shots and crosses from his team-mates. He looked a few pounds overweight and not very fit.

'Fuck off, Fat Arse!' yelled the bloke next to me. 'Oi, Fatso, I'm talking to you!' But the keeper wisely chose not to rise to the bait and look round at who was abusing him.

The Chelsea players ran out and it seemed everyone in this end wanted to let the team know that we were there to support them.

'Ipswich, Ipswich!' could be heard coming from the back of the terrace. Everyone looked round and the chants were soon drowned out by roars of 'Chelsea, Chelsea!' Nevertheless, it told us that the Ipswich boys were in here somewhere.

At half-time we went and got a cup of Bovril. All the talk among the Chelsea faces was about where the Ipswich chanting was coming from. Eccles decided to have a wander through the crowd to see if he could locate the Ipswich fans. We tagged along with him and about fifty of his posse as he pushed through the spectators. We stood right at the back under the covered terrace as Eccles surveyed the mass of heads. I'd seen him do this many times, especially at Stamford Bridge where he'd have one eye on the game and the other on the look-out for any signs of infiltration by enemy forces. I stood on my tiptoes but all I could see was a mass of checked shirts and Fred Perrys and the bristles of a thousand of crewcut bonces basking in the sun.

The referee whistled and signalled the end of the game. Everyone pushed towards the exits. As we got out onto the street the crowd in front of me stopped. People were pushing and leaning back. A large circle had formed with two men standing in the middle. A black man in a green army jacket who looked about twenty was facing our main man. Behind the black guy were a dozen or so other dark faces. They were all shouting instructions to their man, who, despite being heavily outnumbered, remained relatively calm.

The crowd were baying for blood, wanting some action. 'Do him! Do him!' one of them shouted.

Someone on our side shouted similar encouragement to our boy. Our man had his arms down by his sides. He took off his brown suede bomber jacket and stood there in a dark-blue Fred Perry and white Levi's Sta-prest. The black fella looked like a GI from Vietnam in his green combat jacket. The crowd were getting restless and started to push forward. He did some strange arm movements, twisting and flicking his hands in our man's face. I'd seen Morris dancers at the hospital garden fête do something like that.

'What the fuck is that all about?' I asked Jeff.

'He's doing some Kung Fu moves, I think,' he said.

By the look of things, he'd mesmerised our man, who hadn't moved an inch. The crowd on both sides could wait no longer and what was a one-on-one turned into a free-for-all as people started trading kicks and punches. The Ipswich boys backed off but tried to make a stand on the corner of the street. The sheer weight of the Chelsea mob forced the Ipswich fans back down the road, though. The Old Bill came in on horseback and this gave our opponents the chance to regroup. Chelsea took the initiative again and charged at Ipswich, who stood their ground and had a go.

A police horse reared up into the air and everyone did their best to avoid getting trampled by the frightened beast, its rider just managing to stay on.

More fights broke out on the other side of the street and the Old Bill did their best to get across there and stop it. They nicked a few people and dragged them off. Chelsea were driving the Ipswich mob backwards. Our extra numbers were beginning to tell and it was like a dam bursting when the Old Bill and the Ipswich fans were finally overrun. Some of our boys had armed themselves with pieces of wood from a fence they'd just ripped down and they chased a group of Ipswich fans up a side street. Our mob had split in to small gangs and we wandered the streets looking for their boys, all of whom had disappeared completely. All we saw were other Chelsea boys prowling around. Pretty soon everyone got bored and drifted back to the main road. It was deserted. A car drove past and 'Cockney wankers!' was shouted out of the window by the brave person in the passenger seat.

The fighting was all finished as law and order were restored. The Old Bill and their dogs came in and herded us towards the station, marching us through the streets like an army. We knew there would be no Ipswich fans waiting at the station for one last ruck. They'd done their bit outside the ground and, to give them their due, they had put up a good show. There were two things we knew the good people of Ipswich liked – bingo and Kung Fu.

Back in Mitcham, we stopped in Hutton's fish-and-chip shop, but instead of the usual takeaway we treated ourselves to a meal in the restaurant. Nothing lavish – just steak-and-kidney pie – but it was on a plate and it was hot. The others couldn't work out why I'd got a bigger portion than them. I didn't tell them it was because Steve Harris's mum, Rosie, worked there as a waitress and that her other part-time job was cleaning at the town hall with my mum. I was in two minds whether to phone Lynda. It was a bit late and her mum might get the hump. Still, no doubt I'd see her tomorrow. We headed off home and on the way passed Wilke's, Hutton's local rivals in the fish-and-chip trade. One of us pushed the door open.

'Got any chips left?'

'Yes,' replied the woman behind the counter.

'Well, you shouldn't have cooked so many,' we all shouted at once as we slammed the door and bombed up the road, laughing.

I said goodnight to the others and turned into Gas Works Alley. I bumped straight into a young couple snogging up against the wall. I apologised for disturbing them and, as they broke away, I saw that the girl in the romantic clinch was Lynda's mate, Pauline. She gave me a dirty look and got back to tickling the bloke's tonsils.

'That girl has had more pricks than I've had hot dinners,' I laughed to myself. 'She's been engaged more times than the local telephone exchange. And she's got the cheek to think I'm not good enough for Lynda. Jealous, that's all she fucking is.'

The next day Lynda turned up at the rec and after a game of football we sat around and talked about the trip to Ipswich.

'Tell all the boys about those birds we met in the café,' Tony said to me.

Lynda stared at me with daggers. 'Come here, Martin King, I want a word with you.'

'Can't it wait?' I said, 'I'm with me mates.'

She came up behind me, got me in a headlock and dragged me away. She certainly knew how to embarrass me. I was turning scarlet. Everyone was looking and I felt such a div.

'What's all this about cafés and girls?' she demanded as she dumped me down on the grass. Just to make sure I couldn't get away, she pinned me down flat with her knees on my shoulders. Had she been watching the wrestling on telly?

'It's me or football, the choice is yours,' she said. 'I'll give you until tomorrow to make up your mind. And by the way, thanks for the promised phone call you didn't bother to make. Don't give me the excuse that you were late back because you were seen and you know who by.'

She got to her feet and called Pauline over, who sneered at me, and the pair of them walked away.

I brushed myself down, and felt all the boys' eyes on me.

I didn't need another twenty-four hours to make up my mind. I walked over and rejoined my mates.

'All right, Mart?'

'Yeah, fine,' I smiled. 'I'm looking forward to going to football next week. Who've we got?'

NINE

The Long Good Friday

Back at school on the Monday I let the word get around the girls that I was now available and back on the dating scene, once again young, free and single. Lynda was history, although I had her to thank for losing my virginity.

She came to my house one day when the old man was at work and Mum was at bingo. I'd done just about everything else to her but we hadn't yet gone all the way at that point – until she dragged me up to my bedroom, took all my clothes off and pulled me on top of her naked body. I said she stripped me naked but in fact I still had my socks on and a lime-green Ben Sherman shirt.

It was over in seconds and afterwards I wondered what it was all about – was that it? Was that what everyone talked about at school? 'Now I've done it, I don't know if I'll be doing it again,' I thought to myself. 'I can't say I didn't enjoy it, but what's all the fuss about? Still, how many kids who say they've shagged a bird are telling the truth? At least I'm a real man now. I've sown my wild oats, and it makes me feel almost grown up.'

I didn't really tell anyone what I'd been up to, just in case word got back to Mum. I didn't think she would care that her little soldier had had his first bunk-up. What would bother her, though, was the fact that I'd had someone to the house without letting her know first so she could tidy up and do the housework. She'd be sick if she thought someone had perhaps seen the place in a mess. She would hate it if people thought her home was a dirty hole. She was always the first one to slag anyone else off. If she visited someone else's home, her face would light up if she saw a speck of dust or where the hoover had missed a bit, so she couldn't let her guard down. She had standards to maintain, rules to stick to and appearances to keep up.

The talk at school that week was of the friendly between Chelsea and Arsenal being played on Friday evening at the National Athletics Stadium at Crystal Palace. It struck us as an odd venue and a bit of a strange day for a match – most games were on a Saturday or midweek. A lot of kids from school seemed up for it, though, and it was only a few miles away, so it would be easy to get to. I think it was more a reserve-team fixture then anything too serious. The Spurs lads from school had aligned themselves to Chelsea, due to their hatred of the Gooners. The West Ham and Palace fans said they'd be in the Arsenal corner. Spurs and Chelsea joining up – it was unheard of. 'This will be a first, if it happens,' I thought. 'I'd rather join the Girl Guides than the Yids.'

A meet was arranged for five o'clock on the day of the game outside The Greyhound, a big old pub opposite Streatham Common. Our plan was to catch a train to Crystal Palace station, which was right next door to the stadium. The majority of our lot were assembled before five o'clock, apart from, of course, the Spurs fans, who, surprise surprise, failed to show. The twenty or so lads who had turned up headed off for the train station. We stood around chatting, not really knowing what to expect. Would Arsenal have a few boys out tonight?

The train pulled in and we jumped on. It was standing room only. We got talking to a few lads who, thankfully, turned out to be Chelsea boys – we hadn't a clue who'd be on it when we jumped aboard. They told us that the previous train from central London was packed with Arsenal's firm, so it looked like it could turn out to be an eventful evening. I just hoped some of our top boys would be there.

When we arrived at Crystal Palace and the whole train emptied out, it looked like we had a good mob. We started chanting 'Chelsea!' and that gave everyone a bit more confidence and a feeling of togetherness. We made our way out of the station and headed towards the stadium. There was no one hanging around outside.

With more chants of 'Chelsea!', our confidence soared. We paid to get in and made our way towards the Chelsea fans who'd congregated at the far side of the ground. To my surprise the place was nearly full. It was odd to see Chelsea playing in what was basically an athletics stadium. The Arsenal fans were at the opposite end to us and the numbers looked about even. A couple of fellas from Battersea told us there was a bit of a stand-off with an Arsenal mob just outside the main gates. I didn't spot many coppers on duty.

'We squared up to them and they walked towards us,' the lad said. 'A few punches were thrown and for some reason our lot backed off. Arsenal's boys kept coming forward and we started to disintegrate. One minute we're up for a row, next thing just half a dozen of us are facing this Arsenal firm. It was humiliating, and if wasn't for the Old Bill coming between us, we would have got mollered. Let's hope we do better if we run into them after the game.'

I was beginning to think I might have made a mistake coming here tonight. I could have been at the youth club over at Phipps Bridge, dancing to Jimmy Cliff while he sang about a 'Wonderful World, Beautiful People'. At this moment in time I wasn't feeling too clever and the people around me were anything but beautiful.

I noticed that a few older lads from Pollards Hill were trying to organise the Chelsea mob. Prof, a small bloke who was well known from the Shed end, came over to Smudger Smith, the self-elected leader of today's mob. Prof had his little round pebble glasses dangling from one ear. His trademark white butcher's coat with the players' names and 'CFC' painted all over it, had been ripped and torn, the collar and one sleeve hanging in shreds. He had tears streaming down his cheeks and snot blowing from his nose.

'Smudger, Smudger!' shouted Prof, pushing his way through the crowd. 'Look what them Arsenal bastards have done to me.'

I turned away, trying not to laugh.

'Them bastards just attacked me,' said Prof, trying to stem the flow of tears. 'I was at the hotdog stand when a dozen Arsenal skins came up behind me and started taking the piss out of my coat. I turned round but before I could say anything one of them punched me on the nose!'

More stifled laughter from me. I hated that creepy little wanker. 'Serves you right, you little arsehole,' I said aloud, but no one was listening. 'You give it the big one at Chelsea, hanging around with Greenaway and Eccles, but really you're nothing. You're about twenty-five, four foot tall, going bald, with Tizer-bottle-bottom glasses. Fucking idiot. I expect you were gobbing off, if the truth were known.' With him, though, this Arsenal mob's existence was debatable.

'Leave it with me,' said Smudger Smith, the temporary leader, 'I'll get all the boys together and at half-time we will go down to the tea stall and sort this out.'

'How long till half-time?' I asked the geezer next to me.

'Ten minutes,' he said.

I decided to get out before anyone else and do a bit of scouting and see if I could find this Arsenal lot. I made my way out onto the grass bank behind the main stand and, sure enough, some Arsenal boys were hanging around the tea stall. As I walked towards them they were all screwing at me for some reason. I carried on walking towards them. 'Turn back!' I was telling myself, but my legs weren't listening. 'Turn back, turn back!' the voice in my head was saying, but my legs had taken over my senses and were propelling me on. I found myself right in amongst the Arsenal and all eyes were on me. I picked one face out of the crowd and nodded my head. 'All right mate!' stumbled from my lips. The bloke looked at me blankly, 'Say something, please!' screamed the voice in my head.

The bloke half smiled. 'Hello, Shorty,' the fella said, and all his mates laughed.

Yes, yes, yes, yes, yes! Bingo, I was in with their boys.

'Tea, please, guv,' I said to the man on the stall, slapping a coin on the tea-soaked counter. I nervously took a sip from the boiling plastic cup and it burnt my lips. 'Fucking hell, that's hot,' I said to myself, casting a glance round to check no one had noticed me scalding myself. Now that I was behind enemy lines, I took a good look about. I was standing next to some blokes. They must have been about thirty years old. A couple looked even older – probably my dad's age. I couldn't imagine the old man rucking at football, though I'd seen him get quite upset at the wrestling on the telly – not with the wrestlers but with the old girls in the crowd who'd leap from their seats in the front row and lash out with their rolled-up umbrellas at the wrestlers in the ring.

'They're only acting, you silly old cows!' he'd scream at the telly.

'Well, if they're only acting, Dad, why are you getting so upset?'

Dad loved his wrestling. He even watched it live a couple of times a week and he wouldn't miss it for the world when it was on telly on a Saturday afternoon. No one was allowed to talk when it was on.

The Arsenal mob had a few kids my age with them but the majority were grown men, whereas our mob were mostly young kids with a few older lads leading. None of our top boys had turned up so it looked like a pasting was on the cards. By the sound of it, though, the Arsenal boys were not really out for trouble. How wrong can you be? Within seconds the mood of the crowd had changed.

'Here we go, Johnny,' shouted one of the Arsenal boys, nodding towards the Chelsea mob who'd come down from the terrace and were ganging up on the grass bank just in front of us. Seeing what was going on, more Arsenal fans poured down from the terraces and swelled the mob standing round the tea stall.

A big smile lit up Johnny's face. 'Here we go, boys!' he said and walked towards the Chelsea mob. The faithful crowd behind him matched him step for step. I shifted out of the Arsenal front line and positioned myself on the sidelines. If it was a tug-of-war between the two sides, the position I'd taken up was where the referee would stand.

A few of the Chelsea boys began to bounce up and down and motion the Arsenal fans towards them. 'No need to do that, boys,' I thought, 'they're coming your way anyway.' Chelsea charged at the Arsenal mob but stopped ten foot short. There was more bouncing about from our lot. Johnny's grin was even bigger. He landed a punch on a Chelsea fan's nose and the bloke went down. 'Fucking hell!' I thought. 'Keep out of his way, he's got a dig on him.' Cue mass panic as the Chelsea boys turned and ran. Not one of our lot stood and Arsenal chased the Chelsea mob back onto the terraces.

An Arsenal skinhead in his twenties grabbed my Harrington jacket by the collar, screwed it round with his fist and lifted me up off the floor. 'Who you with, you little squirt?' he snapped, lifting me higher. I was looking down on his cropped hair and I noticed his cut-in parting wasn't quite straight. I decided I'd better not tell him. It would only upset him and he was angry enough already. He dropped me flat out on to the ground and he pulled his leg back ready to kick me. Just as I braced myself for a size ten Dr Marten boot to make contact with my head, from above me I heard a voice say, 'Stop, stop, he's with us!' and an Arsenal fan bent down and helped me to my feet. The gorilla grunted and walked off, his knuckles scraping along the ground.

'Thanks, mate,' I said to my saviour, as I straightened my jacket and brushed myself down. The big skinhead turned back and glared at me. I smiled at him and he almost growled. It must have been payback time for me laughing at Prof's misfortune. I made myself scarce and melted into the crowd. Two coppers arrived with dogs and pushed the Arsenal fans back onto the terrace and I slipped back in amongst the Chelsea fans, hoping no one saw me with the Arsenal mob.

One of the older fellas from Pollards Hill had a right shiner of a black eye. An inquest was being held into why Chelsea shit out so easily. Smudger looked cheesed off as temporary leader after just one day in office.

He tried to assert some authority as he addressed his weary troops, whose lack of interest was obvious. 'All we got to do is stick together when we get outside,' he was saying. 'If we do that we've got half a chance. The only other solution is we fuck off before the end of the game and hope the Old Bill give us an escort or we drift away singly and hope we don't get picked off.'

Now I was really shitting myself. I'd never been with a Chelsea mob who seemed so worried. One of the older lot interrupted Smudger. 'No, fuck it,' he said, 'we've got to stay together,' and everyone nodded in agreement. 'It's our only hope of getting out in one piece.'

Ten minutes before the end and it looked like some of our lot had thought better of it and were starting to drift away. They'd chosen self-preservation. I could see Arsenal had made their minds up and were already mobbing up on the grass bank. 'What do I do?' I said to myself. 'Should I try to sneak out and go it alone, or will there be safety in numbers?' I couldn't see any of my mates from school, though knowing some of those yellow-bellied bastards, they'd be home by now. I supposed they fucked off after the skirmish at half-time. I looked around and realised I didn't really know anyone in this Chelsea mob. I was with total strangers. I spotted Smudger Smith heading for the exit alone. I guessed he'd handed in his resignation. He never reigned very long, the cowardly wanker. It was no good electing yourself leader if you weren't going to have a fight.

The game ended and we started to leave the stadium. No one spoke. I wondered what had happened to the policy of the big fellas at the front. A solitary copper with a dog tried to force the Arsenal mob back as they walked menacingly towards us. He gave the snarling dog plenty of leash and it jumped and growled at anybody within biting distance. The Arsenal boys didn't seem put out by the dog and just walked on either side of it and continued towards us. Our numbers had dwindled to about fifty faces. This was the worst mob I'd ever seen.

'Stand, Chelsea, stand!' someone shouted but half our mob were on their toes. I looked around and saw the railway station was only two hundred yards away. Everyone had the same idea and we made a dash for safety. I glanced over my shoulder and the Arsenal mob were on our tails. They'd broken through what coppers there were. Suddenly, the crowd in front of me came to a grinding halt. The police had closed the gates to the station to allow the people already on the platform to get on the first train that arrived. There was little alternative but to turn and face the Arsenal fans who by now were right on top of us. It was fight or get a kicking, we'd no option. I saw grown men nearly in tears before they'd even been hit. It was total chaos as people rushed around in every direction.

It was toe-to-toe stuff, and there were a few bloody noses on our side as Arsenal came steaming in. One of them hit me over the head with a rolled-up umbrella. I bet he was a wrestling fan. I ducked behind a tall Chelsea skinhead who was doing really well and landing some decent punches. I wished we'd more like him – he wasn't scared to get stuck in. Even the Arsenal boys didn't want to get too close – they knew this kid could fight. He was probably a good amateur boxer by the look of it. *Crack!* There goes another bone in someone's nose. Down went another Gooner.

'Go on, son!' I said from behind him, 'Go on, you're doing well!'

The Old Bill arrived with dogs and the Arsenal fans backed off. The metal gates to the station were opened and everyone pushed inside. Nearly everyone made it but a few of us were left outside. The Arsenal fans seized this opportunity to attack again, launching bricks and bottles in our direction. You couldn't see the missiles in the darkness but you could hear them shattering against the station's metal fence. A bloke behind me got hit in the face with a brick. Another brick just missed me and I heard it whizz past my ear. More and more people from our side were getting hit.

I made up my mind to get out of there when I saw a copper get injured. Self-preservation kicked in. I jumped onto the roof of a parked car and pulled myself on to the station roof. I clambered along and jumped down into the park. As I walked through the darkness I could hear the noise of the fighting fading behind me. I made my way up towards the main road at the top of Crystal Palace. Police sirens and blue flashing lights filled the night air. A man walking his dog threw a comment about 'bloody hooligans'. I climbed out onto the road as police cars raced past me. I pulled my collar up and tried to blend in with the crowds milling about. A pub-full of people came out to see what was going on. The racket had disturbed their Friday-night boozing. I overheard more comments about hooligans and drink and spells in the army. 'Do their parents know where they are?' said one.

Just when I began to feel safe, a voice boomed out behind me. 'Oi, pipsqueak!'

For some unknown reason I looked around. It was my skinhead mate with the wonky parting. I took off like a shot as he and his mates gave chase. I dodged in and out of the crowds. I knew he was not far behind me and I could hear him shouting, 'Stop that kid, someone stop him!' I reached the end of the road and spotted a bus that had got stuck in the traffic. I jumped on and ran upstairs. It pulled away and I was safe. I wiped the sweat from my brow and unzipped my jacket. My heart was pounding. I didn't even know where the bus was going and I had to ask the conductor.

'Croydon!' he said and I handed him my fare. From Croydon I could catch a bus to Mitcham. To be honest I wouldn't have cared if the bus had been heading for Brighton, I was just glad to get away. 'Fucking hell, that was some row back there,' I said to myself. 'I hope my mate, the big skinhead, ain't still chasing the bus.' I wiped the steamed-up window to check. There was no sign of him. No, unless he was sitting downstairs, I was safe and sound and going home in one piece.

That Monday morning Mum came in and woke me up for school. I'd done my paper round and climbed back into my bed.

'I ain't going to school today,' I told her, 'I don't feel well.'

'It's up to you, boy,' she replied. Some days it didn't seem to bother her if I went to school or not – I think she was just glad of the company. There was no way I was showing my face to those gloating Gooners, and the rest of the Spurs and Palace and West Ham wankers. I'd give them a day or so to forget and then I'd face them, but until then a spot of shopping with Mum at Tooting Market would do me.

TEN

Swatting the Hornets

'Hold it there, lads,' called the policeman out of his car window as he pulled up alongside us. He got out and walked over to us. 'Where you off to at this time of day? It's five o'clock in the morning,' he said, looking at his watch.

We told him we were walking to Wimbledon Station and then taking the train to Fulham Broadway to queue for tickets for the FA Cup semi-final between Chelsea and Watford – that's if they hadn't sold out already.

'I'm a Chelsea fan, all my family are Chelsea fans,' said the copper. 'Come on, jump in and I'll run you to the station.' Jeff , Tony and I piled into the back of the police car. 'We're doing well this season,' said the copper, 'I fancy us to win the cup,' and he waffled on about team tactics and how lazy Osgood was and that if he showed a bit more commitment and enthusiasm he would be a regular England international. 'Trouble is, he won't run for the ball, he wants it right at his feet. But if he plays well I reckon we'll win the cup.'

'Hope so,' we all said. 'We ain't won nothing in the way of silverware since we've been going. It would shut a lot of kids up at our school if we ran around Wembley with the cup,' added Tony.

I began to daydream. I could see Chopper Harris walking up the steps at Wembley, he receives the gleaming silver pot with blue and white ribbons hanging from the handles from the Queen. He shakes her hand and bows his head then turns towards the Chelsea faithful packed on the noisy terraces and lifts the cup above his head. As he does so I turn to my dad who's standing next to me. He hugs me. 'We've done it, son,' he says as he wipes a tear from his eye. 'I never thought I'd live to see this day. It's one of the proudest days of my life!'

'Steady on, Dad. The way you're talking you'd think I'd scored the winning goal! It's only a dream so perhaps I have.'

My dream was interrupted by someone talking and I came back to reality. 'To tell you the truth,' said the young copper, 'when I saw you three walking up the road in the darkness I thought you'd been up to no good.'

'What, us?' I said, giving him that butter-wouldn't-melt-in-our-mouths look.

But he certainly knew his football and he talked about playing for the police team and trying to emulate his favourite player, Charlie Cooke. Charlie was a one-off. 'The bloke's a genius, his ball skills are something else,' he told us.

Tony and I looked at each other. Fucking hell, we were wondering. How do you shut this guy up? He must be very lonely – they say coppers haven't got any friends. He can't have anyone to speak to. He certainly bent our earholes. He dropped us off right outside the station and wished us well. 'Be lucky, lads, and stay out of trouble,' he shouted as he pulled away. Being in the back of that police car had certainly made me feel nervous and on edge. If anybody we knew had seen us, we would have been branded police informers. You know how these rumours start. Still, he was a good bloke. 'He knows the score,' I said to Jeff, and he and Tony agreed.

We caught the first train out on the District Line and, to our surprise, it was almost empty. 'I thought there'd be thousands going up there early to queue up for tickets,' I said. 'Perhaps they went on sale last week.' My feeble joke got no response.

'The box office doesn't open until ten o'clock, and anyway, we don't know how many have queued overnight,' said Jeff, trying to get a bit of shut-eye.

When we arrived at the ground there were only about a thousand people in the queue. The problem was we'd another four hours before the ticket office opened. We joined the back of the queue, which stretched as far down as the Bovril entrance about three hundred yards away. Jeff decided to take a walk along the queue to see if he knew anyone nearer the front, hoping we might be able to push in with them. He came back ten minutes later – no luck. Some people up ahead had come well prepared with sleeping-bags and little camping stoves on which they were cooking themselves fried breakfasts. It smelled so good – talk about making you feel hungry. Some were swigging from shiny metal hipflasks, others were pouring tea from a thermos and playing cards at little foldaway stools like the ones used for fishing.

After half an hour we were bored shitless. I thought of the nice warm bed I left to come and stand here. What was up with me? Mum was right, I must have been a bit touched. 'Only another three and half hours to go,' I said, looking at my watch.

The man next to me had a transistor radio pressed tightly to his ear. I moved closer to try to hear what radio station he was tuned in to. He was dressed in a nylon anorak and had big grey turn-ups on his Tesco Bomber jeans. He looked like a bit of a trainspotter so I reckoned he was probably listening to something like Radio Two. I imagined the Jimmy Young Show would have been right up his street. He gave me a strange look so I moved even nearer. 'This is the shipping forecast for Sunday the blah, blah, blah.' Fucking shipping forecast he was listening to! That must come in handy when you're standing in a street in west London, queuing for football tickets. I wondered what the weather was like in Bognor. He turned away from me and transferred the radio to his other ear, so I couldn't hear anything. Fucking idiot! I didn't want to hear his stupid radio anyway. It was only because I was bored. 'Poke it up your arse!' I said to him and he looked at me as if he hadn't a clue about what was going on. He moved away from me.

The smell of food being cooked was really getting to us. My belly was rumbling.

'Wish we'd brought my stove I use for fishing,' moaned Tony.

'Wish I'd brought the old man's flask,' I added. We looked at one bloke as he tucked into his eggs and bacon. 'How fucking boring! I ain't doing this again, I hate queuing. Two hours to go!' I said as I checked my watch for the three-hundredth time.

Jeff took another stroll, this time to see how long the queue was behind us. 'You ain't going to believe this!' he said when he came back, 'but the queue is now past Fulham Broadway Station. There are thousands and thousands of people behind us now.'

'I thought you was a long time,' I grumbled, 'you've been gone about fifteen minutes.'

'Well, I had to find a shop that was open,' he replied, throwing me and Tony a Mars Bar each. Our faces lit up and we near enough swallowed them whole we were so hungry.

'Cheers, Jeff!' smiled Tony.

'Anything to relieve the boredom.'

A policeman came along and asked people to keep to the path. We were about twenty-deep across the pavement and spilling out onto the road, making it difficult for the traffic to get past. A couple of cars blew their hooters. 'Busy bastard!' shouted one bloke.

The copper stopped and gave an icy glare at the sea of faces. He wasn't sure who'd said it. 'I'm only doing my job,' he said to no one in particular, as the crowd stared blankly back at him.

'Piss off and open the fucking box office!' someone shouted from behind, but this time the copper kept on walking.

A man in a white coat came along selling the Sunday papers. He was doing a brisk trade but sold out before he got to us. 'That's it,' he said to the hoards of hands waving money at him. 'I've none left.'

'That's what we should do,' I said to the others. 'The next time Chelsea have a big game and we know people will be queuing for tickets, we should get some big flasks and fill them with hot tea and come down here and sell it. Tony, you could bring your camping stove and cook eggs and bacon to sell, and Jeff could go and see Ginger in the newagent's, buy some papers off of him at trade price and sell them to the queue. We'd make a small fortune.'

The others agreed it was a good idea that could well be a money-making scam for the future. We were always on the look-out for ways to make a few quid.

At last the queue started to move and within an hour we were clutching our semi-final tickets. The game was to be played at White Hart Lane, home of Tottenham Hotspur, our arch rivals. There was no love lost between the two clubs since Spurs beat us in the Cup final a few years ago. I'd been to White Hart Lane many times with the Chelsea mob, but playing against Watford there would be different. Watford were in a lower division and their fans were unknown to us. Rumours started to fly that the Spurs boys would be turning out on the day and teaming up with Watford.

Everyone I spoke to around south London seemed to have a ticket for the game. The Chelsea firm had arranged to meet at Fulham Broadway and on the day of the match thousands of Chelsea boys turned up for the meet. All the pubs were open early and packed to the rafters, and every known thug in south and west London was there. The massive mob decided to move off, though no one knew what would be the next port of call. We were on one of the first trains out of Fulham Broadway and we went with hundreds of others to Tower Hill Station. Once there, we poured out onto the streets. Eccles, the main man, took control of the mob. No one knew our destination as we strolled through the deserted streets which would normally have been filled with office workers. We were deadly quiet as we snaked in and out of the back streets. A couple of down-and-outs tucked up in cardboard boxes were woken from their sleep, their scruffy dog's barking alerting them to our presence. Security guards came to the doors of their office blocks to see what was going on. We crossed main roads and then back down side streets. It was a real Magical Mystery Tour. What would be at the end of this journey into the unknown? A mob of Watford? A Spurs firm? It was none of those, as soon became apparent as Liverpool Street Station came into view. Word was passed back from those at the front that we would all be catching a train from here to White Hart Lane Station.

'What was all that about?' I asked Jeff as we stood on the platform waiting for the train to arrive.

'Fuck knows!' he replied with a shrug of his shoulders.

'I can't believe that!' said one skinhead wiping the sweat from his brow with his Chelsea scarf.

The train pulled in and a mad rush ensued as everyone clambered for a seat. By the time the doors were shut and it was ready to leave, we were packed inside like sardines. Someone from British Rail made a decision not to stop at any stations along the way, and we went straight through to White Hart Lane. The train was rocking from side to side as the strains of 'Knees Up Mother Brown' echoed through the carriages. When we reached our destination, we were met by lines of policemen all along the platform. The train doors opened and its contents spilled out. In the rush people were falling over and others were tripping over them. One or two were sprawled out on the floor. The police charged in, thinking a fight had broken out, but it was just high spirits.

The mass of bodies moved out onto the Tottenham High Road and the atmosphere alone told you this was no ordinary game. We were just one win away from Wembley. There were Chelsea fans everywhere and we seemed to be in the majority. I noticed the odd one or two Watford fans but none who looked like they were up for a ruck. We reached the Paxton Road end of the ground where a few Watford supporters were already queuing to get in. Our tickets were for the Park Lane end, which was normally home to the Spurs supporters. We walked down to our end, hoping some Yids would be waiting for us, but there was no sign of any. Everyone walked back down the other side, the size of the Chelsea mob growing with every step. We walked all the way around the ground and found ourselves back at the Watford end.

'Right, lads,' said a senior police officer, 'you've seen all there is to see, so I suggest you go back to your own end of the stadium.' He held his arms out at his sides like a shepherd pushing his sheep in a certain direction. A few other coppers joined in and copied their governor's action. Within minutes the police had the Paxton Road end sealed off. A few Watford fans decided that they were safe now so they stuck two fingers up and gave the Chelsea mob the wanker sign. Our boys weren't going to take shit like that from a two-bob mob like Watford who hadn't even been seen all day. The thin blue line was swept away as the Chelsea mob surged towards the Watford fans. I was at the front and I was carried along by the sheer weight of numbers. As I was being pushed along the pavement, I caught a glimpse of a hippy-looking bloke in a denim cap and a tatty jean jacket up ahead. He was sitting there busking with a guitar, singing a Bob Dylan song about love and peace. A dog-end or maybe a joint hung from his lips.

'Fuck me, Mr Folk Singer, but if you don't get up off that pavement, you're going to get crushed in the stampede,' I told him as I managed to break free of the crowd. The few coins people had thrown to him were already being kicked along the path. Standing next to the bewildered-looking bloke were two young kids aged about ten and twelve. Both had Watford rosettes pinned to their chests. Without stopping to think I scooped the pair of them up and jumped into the safety of a shop doorway. I stood in front of them for protection and could feel their little hearts thumping as they clung to the backs of my legs. They were shaking with fright.

As the last of the mob surged past, I turned and asked if they were all right. It seemed they were just shaken by their ordeal.

'Thanks, mister,' they both said. 'You saved our lives.'

Their father was picking up his scattered coins from the kerb. He came over, shaking his head. 'Thanks, mate, you saved my boys from getting seriously hurt.' He shook my hand and stuffed the few coins he'd managed to retrieve into his torn denims.

'What're your names?' I asked the two boys as I bent down to wipe the tears off the little fat one's cheeks.

'I'm Dougie,' said the little podgy one.

'And I'm Eddie,' said the tall skinny one.

'Do me a favour,' I said to the pair of them, 'never get involved in any of this football violence. It's not the sort of place young kids like you should be.'

'We won't,' they both said.

'When you go to school on Monday and your teacher asks you to write an essay about what you did at the weekend,' I told them, 'write about what you saw today.'

They both promised they would never get involved in fighting at football and would just write about it instead.

Before I went, I nipped into the shop we were standing outside and I bought them a little present each. I got the fat one a model aircraft, a Spitfire fighter, and the skinny one a joke book. Their eyes lit up but the fat one did make me laugh when he asked if I'd bought them sweets as well. Greedy little bastard.

'Thanks a lot, mister,' they said as they jumped up and down with excitement.

'Poor little fuckers,' I thought, 'I hope they won't be affected by what's gone on today.' To this day I often wonder what happened to those two kids.

I walked around the ground and soon spotted Tony and Jeff. They were worried I'd been nicked or injured and carted away in a ambulance. I told them the story of the two kids and as usual they were very sympathetic. 'Should have left them to get crushed,' said Jeff. 'I've got a cousin who lives in Luton and he fucking hates Watford. He went over there the other week with a crowd of his mates to a disco in a youth club. A fight started and one of his mates got hit over the head with a bottle. They went back a week later with the numbers more even and the cowardly bastards locked themselves in and wouldn't come out. The police arrived and threatened arrests if the mob didn't disperse. Brave or what?'

We made our way into the ground and stood near the corner flag where the Park Lane met the Shelf. Behind me I could hear Eccles organising a trip behind enemy lines. 'Tommy!' he shouted to someone in the crowd, 'give me fifty men, we're going up the Watford end in search of Yids or to see what Watford have to offer!'

'Count me in,' I said and took up my position next to the general. Tommy pointed at people in the crowd and they stepped forward, and then we were off. I kept my eye on the leader's brown suede jacket. I knew that if I stayed within spitting distance of him I wouldn't go far wrong. We ducked in and out of the crowds. People moved out of the way to let us past. We were on a mission and even though I was only a volunteer and hadn't been handpicked by Sergeant Tommy, I was still part of this.

We came to the Paxton Road terrace where a few Watford fans, seeing our arrival, scurried down to the front to get away. A big bloke in a dark-brown sheepskin stood his ground. One of our lot nutted him in the face and he went down, no longer a threat. The Watford crowd behind the goal moved towards us. A black guy in amongst them was pointed out by one of our lot as a main face at Tottenham. We charged down the terraces towards them, ducking under the crush barriers, and the two mobs clashed. Fists and boots flew and the Old Bill rushed in to break up the fighting. A few blokes from both sides were arrested and carted away around the edge of the pitch and out of sight down the tunnel from which the two teams were due to emerge any minute now.

Our platoon headed back to our own end. I stood next to Eccles as he got a victor's reception. There wouldn't be a repeat performance because the Old Bill had strung a line of coppers along the top to the bottom of the halfway line.

This was Chelsea's tenth FA Cup semi-final appearance. The pitch looked a bit sandy and I worried it might not suit our style of play – we liked to pass the ball around and the heavy pitch might not allow that to happen. My doubts were soon dispelled as goals flowed from Webb, Osgood, Houseman and then Hutchinson with a fourth. Houseman finally finished the rout with his second. The Watford keeper was furious with his defenders. The game ended a convincing five-nil win for Chelsea.

After the match it was party-time with fans packing the pubs around the ground. Others headed off home, dancing all the way up Tottenham High Road. Wembley, here we come!

It was another month before we were due to play Leeds in the final. As the game drew nearer the rush was on for tickets. The boys and I weren't season-ticket-holders and we'd not been collecting the vouchers from the home match programmes, so we didn't really stand a chance of getting tickets for the game. In the end I had to settle for watching it on the telly. Dad and I settled back in our front room to watch the game. Leeds scored first from a weak header by Jack Charlton. Two of our defenders had got in each other's way and the ball trickled over the line. Chelsea equalised through Peter Houseman, whose weak shot somehow squeezed under the diving body of Gary Sprake, the Leeds goalie. Dad and I went bananas, jumping up and down, kissing and hugging one another. Mum came in from the kitchen to see what all the noise was about. 'Silly pair of bastards,' she mumbled as she walked back out.

Our joy was short-lived as Mick Jones, the Leeds centre-forward, put them back in front. Chelsea pressed forward in search of an equaliser. We hit the post and had a chance cleared off the line and it looked like we'd blown it. Dad and I looked at each other. We couldn't speak. We were on the edge of our seats. I was chewing my fingernails and Dad was chewing the end of his pipe. 'Come on, Chelsea!' we both shouted as John Hollins took a free-kick on the edge of the Leeds penalty box. He floated one in and Ian Hutchinson threw himself at the ball and headed into the net at the near post. '*Goal! Fuuuuucccckkkkiiinnnggg beautiful!*' Dad and I danced around the room. We were still celebrating as the referee blew the final whistle.

After the draw at Wembley, the replay was at Old Trafford. Again Dad and I sat at home and watched the match on TV. Mum went off to the bingo. The stadium was packed solid with the bulk of the Chelsea fans behind the goal in the Stretford end. Some of the early tackles from both sides were certainly X-rated. 'If it carries on like this, it'll finish as a five-a-side game,' said Dad. Bonetti, our goalkeeper, was injured as he jumped for a high cross and Jones of Leeds clattered into him. Bonetti's knee had to be heavily strapped. He looked in pain though he carried on, but you could see he was unable to move properly. Leeds scored first, through Jones, who had been constantly booed by the Chelsea faithful. We sat in silence, fearing the worst, until my man Charlie Cooke picked the ball up and floated a pin-point cross on to Ossie's diving head. We went ballistic. I ran out into the back garden and jumped up and down like a lunatic. 'Sit down, boy, for fuck's sake,' smiled the old man. The game ended in a draw and we were into extra time. With just minutes to go Chelsea won a throw-in down by the Leeds penalty area. The chant of 'Chelsea! Chelsea!' echoed round the ground. Ian Hutchinson, our long-throw specialist, picked up the ball. He rubbed it and dried it on his shirt. Charlie Cooke made a darting run and Hutchinson nodded and smiled. There was only one place that ball was going, and he hurled it to the far post. A group of players jumped for it but it skimmed off the top of David Webb's head and into the back of the Leeds net. I went fucking apeshit. The old man sat there, shaking his head. I thought he'd gone into shock. The whistle blew and we'd done it! After sixty-five years of trying, we'd at last won the FA Cup. Ron Harris, the Chelsea captain, wearily trudged up the steps to receive the Cup, not from the Queen, as in my dream, but from some old bald git in glasses who looked about a hundred years old with barely the strength to lift the trophy and hand it over to the jubilant Chelsea skipper. I looked at Dad and saw him wiping the tears from his eyes. 'We done it, boy,' he said, his voice, like his bottom lip, quivering with emotion. I shook his hand and put my arms around him.

Mum came in and told us she'd just won twenty pounds at the bingo. I don't know who was happier.

Before I went to bed I hung my blue-and-white Chelsea scarf out of my bedroom window. I left it there for weeks. On Monday at school the game was replayed in the playground with us Chelsea fans playing the part of our heroes while the defeated Leeds team was made up of the jealous bastards who hated the thought of Chelsea winning anything. The whole of west and south London was on a high for weeks afterwards.

ELEVEN

The Irons

'Yes, madam, how can I help you?'

'We're staying here for a week's holiday!' said Mum.

'Name?' asked the man.

'Mrs King and Martin King, and Mrs Burden and son Kevin Burden.'

The man looked down his list and ticked us off. 'There you go, chalet number 100,' and he handed Mum the key. 'As you leave the reception, go straight across the square and number 100 is facing you. Leave your cases here and I'll have them sent over to you.'

'Not bleeding likely!' retorted Mum. 'All my personal gear's in them cases and I ain't having no one rummaging through my personal effects!'

'But, Mrs King,' he said, 'the man who will deliver the cases is one of our employees.'

'I don't care,' said Mum. 'Come on, Maise,' she said to her sister. 'Oi, Martin, stop laughing and bring them cases.'

I looked at the man and he shrugged his shoulders as if to say 'What was all that about?' We hadn't been there five minutes and already she'd upset the man on the reception. On the coach on the way down she'd had a row with the driver because he wanted a ten-minute stop so everyone could get off and stretch their legs. Mum, however, wanted a half-hour break so she could have something to eat before getting back on the coach. No wonder the old man ducked out of this holiday. He knew just how embarrassing she could be. 'You and the boy go, love. I'm up to me neck in work!' he'd told her. So I got dragged along with her sister and my cousin Kevin. Kev was all right, he wasn't a bad bloke.

We reached our chalet which was on the upper level of a two-storey block. 'Put the kettle on, Maise!' said Mum as she dropped her bag just inside the door. She slumped back onto the settee. 'I'm fucking cream-crackered,' she announced.

'Don't worry about me!' I said, 'I've only lugged a suitcase half way round the world and then up them stairs!' She was so selfish, she only ever thought of herself.

'Before you make the tea, Maise, give that boy a medal!' she called.

'Let's check out the lie of the land,' Kevin suggested. 'Might be some nice birds here.'

Mum overheard. 'While we're on that subject,' she said, 'let me make it quite clear that you are to bring no girls, or "birds" as you call them, into this chalet while we're on holiday! Do I make myself clear, boy?'

Kevin and I headed for the door without answering. We had a scout about and checked out the swimming-pool and the table-tennis and found where the under-sixteens club was.

When we got back to the chalet, Mum and Aunt Maise were on their way out. 'We're off to bingo, so we've left you some money on the table to get yourselves something to eat. We thought since it'd been a long day for us all, we don't want to start cooking. We're both tired, what with the journey and unpacking, so get yourselves some fish and chips.'

'Tired, my arse!' I said, sarcastically.

'Don't talk to your mother like that!' said Maise.

'Well, she ain't too tired to get dolled up to go to bingo,' I retorted. 'She's had time to plaster all that make-up on her face and splash cheap perfume on!'

'See, I knew it!' snapped Mum, 'I knew you would spoil my holiday!'

I grabbed the money off the table, and Kev and I walked across to the fish-and-chip shop. The queue was about fifty deep. I asked the two girls who were in front of us if there was anywhere else to get something to eat. They both laughed. 'No, this is it.'

'What about down in the town?' I asked.

'What town!' they said. 'Once you go out of the Camp gates, there's only the beach and miles and miles of sand. The nearest town is about ten miles away.'

'Have a look at the old dolly behind the counter,' I said. 'I've seen snails move faster than her!' Kev and the two girls laughed. 'We'll be here all night at this rate,' I said.

'Just be patient,' said Kev, but that was easier said than done. My rumbling stomach reminded me I hadn't eaten since we left home early that morning.

The girls told us they'd been here a week already, and that they'd another week to go.

'What's there to do?' I asked, thinking that the place didn't sound too promising.

'Swimming, table-tennis, snooker. There's a disco and football every day,' they said.

'How about shagging?' I asked.

They both went bright red. Kevin winced and quickly changed the subject. After the girls were served and we got our cod and chips, we all sat down at a table together and ate our eagerly awaited grub. It was a long time coming, but it was well worth the wait.

'Anything happening tonight?' I asked, half hoping the girls would invite us back to their rooms for a night of passion.

'There's a disco at eight o'clock for the under-sixteens in the main ballroom. We'll meet you there if you like!'

Kevin and I nodded in agreement and went off to find our mums. They were halfway through a game of bingo and when my mum spotted me coming through the glass door, she waved me away, mouthing the words 'Sling yer hook'.

'Go and get some more money off your old girl, will you, Kev? Only my mum's a bit busy at the moment.'

'Bollocks!' he replied. 'If I go in there, she'll kill me for interrupting her game!'

'Kev, you're such a fucking coward.'

'If you're so brave,' he said, 'you go in and see your old girl.'

'Kev, are you fucking blind? You've just seen her tell me to piss off!'

We had to admit defeat in our attempt to get some money. We turned and started to walk away when I heard a familiar voice shout, '*House!*' We spun round and saw my mum waving her bingo card in the air, a huge smile on her face.

'Let's strike while the iron's hot!' I told Kev and we rushed through the doors. 'Well done, Mum!' I said and she flung her arms around me. She was kissing me all over my face and jumping up and down. The bingo caller announced the size of the prize money. I wiped off the lipstick that Mum had plastered all over my chops.

'*One hundred pounds! One hundred pounds!*' shrieked Mum. 'First night here and I've won a hundred knicker!' She opened her purse and handed me a pound note. 'Go on, boy, have a night out on me!'

The bingo caller's assistant read the numbers back from Mum's cards and confirmed that she had indeed got a full house. A round of applause rippled through the hall from the other campers and Mum stood up and took a bow. She was milking the applause like she'd just won the Nobel peace prize.

Kev and I headed for the thump of the music coming from the ballroom. Just inside the door were the two girls from the chip shop.

'Didn't take you long to meet a girl,' one of them said to me. 'Been snogging, have you?' she asked.

I looked at her blankly. 'What the hell are you on about?'

'Your face,' she said. 'It's covered in lipstick.'

I wiped my fingers across my face and looked at the palm of my hand. 'Shit, the old girl's smothered me boat-race in bright red lipstick and foundation powder,' I thought.

One of the girls took a tissue from her bag, licked it and began to wipe the traces of make-up off. 'Keep still, you big tart,' she said as I tried to wriggle away from her.

'Let's sit down over here,' suggested the other girl. A slow record came on and the girl nearest me asked if I'd care to dance.

'Why not,' I replied and went straight out into the middle of the floor with her. Kev got up and pulled the other one out onto the dance floor, which was completely empty apart from us four. I could feel my cory getting bigger as she pushed her hips towards mine. Her tits were crushed into my chest. 'Fucking hell,' I thought, 'I'm dancing with three legs. She must know I've got the horn. She must be able to feel the old chap getting bigger by the second.'

I looked at her. 'I don't mean to be rude,' I said, 'but I don't even know your name.'

'I'm Sue and my friend's called Jill.'

'Where you from?' I asked.

'We're both from London.'

'Whereabouts?'

'North London,' she said, 'just down the road from my favourite football team.'

I knew what was coming next. 'It wouldn't be Spurs, would it?' I asked her.

'Well, yes,' she said. 'Are Spurs your team as well?'

There I was, almost having sex with a bird I'd just met. Should I go and spoil it and tell her my team's Chelsea, Spurs' arch enemies? I tried to break the news gently. 'I'm from south London and Kev lives in Surrey.'

'Where's Surrey?' she asked.

'Near London,' I told her.

'Oh, right,' she said. 'So you must be a Chelsea supporter.'

'Are you asking me or telling me?'

'Both,' she replied.

'Come on, let's go for a walk, Kev'll look after Jill.' We made our way out of the door and into the warm evening air. We walked across to the park and sat side by side on the swings, listening to the music floating out through the doors of the ballroom.

'Come on,' she said, 'let's go on the slide together.' I followed her up the metal steps of the slide and admired her lovely tight little arse from behind. She half knew I was looking at her bum and she stopped at the top of the slide, waiting for me to sit down and put my legs on either side of her arse. My dick was now throbbing and I slipped my arms around her waist and pulled her tight against me. We slid down together and came to a halt at the bottom. We unravelled ourselves and I stood up and helped her to her feet. 'Thank you,' she said softly and kissed me on the lips. After a few seconds she pulled away. I swear if that kiss had lasted another few seconds, I would have come in my pants. My bollocks were ready to explode. She took me by the hand. 'Come on, let's do it again.'

As we stood at the bottom of the slide ready to go up, I heard my mum's voice in the darkness. She was heading my way. I grabbed Sue and crouched down under the slide. I put my hand over her mouth and whispered to her to be quiet. She looked at me, puzzled.

Mum passed within a few feet as she and Maise staggered back to the chalet. They seemed well pissed. 'What a fucking night, Maise,' I heard her say. 'First night and I win a hundred pound! Wait till I phone my Fred in the morning – he won't believe it! "Fucking jammy cow," he'll say!'

It sounded like the pair of them had had one too many brandies, as they swayed off into the distance.

Sue and I came out of our hiding place and I explained who Laurel and Hardy were. 'If she'd seen me, I'd never have heard the last of it.'

'Doesn't she like you going with girls, then?' asked Sue.

'No, it's not that. It's just that if she spotted us she would have ripped the piss out of me.'

'Isn't that a bit cruel?' asked Sue.

'Too right,' I said, 'but that wouldn't stop her!'

'Come here,' she said, 'let me give you a hug,' and up came my cory again.

Kevin and Jill eventually found us and we sat chatting about football and our dislike of each other's teams. Jill's parents came looking for them and the girls introduced them to us.

'Thanks for looking after them,' said the dad, giving me and Kevin a sly wink. We both took that as the green light to try to get into the girls' knickers.

'Well, why else would he wink at us?' I said to Kevin as we walked back to the chalet, convinced that this week away was going to be one long bunk-up.

We opened the chalet door and saw that Mum and Maise had fallen into a drunken stupor. The telly was flickering away in the corner and the sound of snoring filled the room. We laughed and left them as we turned in for the night.

Next morning Kev and I were up bright and early to go swimming. Just as we were opening the front door, Mum started to come round. She'd slept on the settee where I'd left her. Maise was curled up in a ball. She opened one eye and then quickly closed it. They both looked in a right old state. I bet they'd spent quite a bit of last night's winnings – they must have been chucking them brandies down their throats.

'Have I been here all night?' Mum asked me.

'We left you exactly where we found you,' I told them both.

'Do us a favour, boy,' groaned Mum, 'any chance of putting the kettle on and making me and your Auntie Maise a nice cup of tea?'

'No chance.' Kevin and I were off out the door with our swimming trunks wrapped up in a towel under our arms. We were no one's skivvies.

'You fucking wait till you want something, you horrible little git,' she yelled after us.

It was only nine o'clock but the swimming-pool was already busy. We swam up and down and had a few dives and jumps off the diving-board but we were starting to get fed up and decided to get out and get dried off. We soon changed our minds when Sue and Jill turned up.

'Over here, girls!' I shouted and they came walking towards us. My dick had shrunk with the cold water, but it soon came back to life when I saw those two in their bikinis.

'Fucking form on them two,' said Kev out of the side of his mouth.

'Morning, girls, care to join us?' I said, patting the edge of the pool to indicate where they should sit down. 'Hope you slept well,' I said to Sue, and didn't dream of me *all* night!'

'You reckon yourself, don't ya,' she replied.

The rest of the day, like the rest of the week, was full of flirting, dancing, playing football and trying damn hard to get my end away. No such luck. On the Friday I decided it was shit or bust. I'd had enough of being nearly there and I wanted to empty my sacks. So I arranged for Sue to come up to the chalet so that we could exchange addresses but I suspected she knew that was all bollocks and that I really wanted to get her up there and rip her drawers off. I told her to come over at about six o'clock, because I knew Mum and Maise would be settling down for a spot of bingo at around that time. Their routine had been the same every night, so my planned bedding of Sue looked as safe as houses.

At ten to six Kev and I were playing football on the grass just outside the chalet. We watched our mums come down the stairs and cross the square and go into the bingo hall. Part one was going according to plan.

'Right, Kev, wait out here, and if your mum or my mum makes a show, let me know straight away. You're my first line of defence, so don't let me down!'

'Trust me,' said Kev.

'You know what our old girls are like – they said they don't trust us and we don't trust them, so they might start thinking we're both up to something. They went off a bit too quiet for my liking tonight,' I said.

'Just get up to the room,' said Kev. 'You're acting paranoid.'

I left Kev kicking the ball up against a wall and went off upstairs. I brushed my teeth and splashed some Hi Karate all over myself. I used to use Brut, of course, but Hi Karate was the aftershave now in fashion. 'Cat's piss,' my dad called it. 'Soap and water, that's what I swear by. A good wash never hurt anyone.'

I picked a clean shirt from the pile of clothes on my bedroom floor and checked myself in the mirror as I buttoned it up. It was a bit creased but it would have to do. The sound of gentle tapping could be heard on the front door. I opened it and Suzy baby was standing there looking absolutely gorgeous. The light-blue make-up on her eyelids really suited her.

'Come on in, nice to see you, make yourself at home.' We both sat down on the edge of my bed. I wasn't going to mess about. I put my arm around her and we both fell backwards onto the bed, our tongues entwined and my hands all over her. I knew this Hi Karate was good stuff. Suddenly she jumped to her feet. Fuck it, every time she felt my rock-hard cory she backed off. She walked towards the window and looked out onto the square below.

'Do you like me, Martin?' she asked, not bothering to look around.

'You know I do,' I told her.

'If I thought you liked me enough, I'd go all the way with you.'

I jumped off the bed, took off my shirt and undid my strides and let them fall to the floor. I ripped my socks off and flung them to the other side of the room. I lay back on the bed in just my pants but she still hadn't turned away from the window. She was saying something about love and trust and how she wanted someone to care for her, not someone who just wanted to use and abuse her. 'I need someone to love me,' she said.

'Oh, yeah, I agree,' I said. She still hadn't clocked I was lying there almost naked.

'Martin,' she said, 'are you listening?'

I jumped up from the bed and put my arms around her. 'Of course I'm listening,' I said. 'Shit, I don't believe it!'

'What's up?' asked Sue, thinking she'd done something wrong.

'See that woman down there waving up at us? Well, that's Kevin's mum, my Auntie Maise. Quick, get out, she looks like she's heading this way.' I pushed Sue out of the door and told her to go along the balcony and take the back staircase. I got dressed quickly and just as I switched the telly on and threw myself on a chair like nothing had been going on, Maise came through front door.

'All right, Maise?' I said, keeping my eyes glued to the telly.

'Where is she?' she demanded.

'Where's who? There's no one here but me.'

'What, do you think I'm fucking daft?' said Maise. 'That girl, where is she?'

'What girl?' I said.

'I saw you looking out of the window,' said Maise. 'I saw the girl with my own eyes. She's got dark hair.' She looked under the bed, checked the bathroom and even glanced under the kitchen table.

I sat there, trying to think of something quick. 'Perhaps you were looking up at next door's window and you saw the couple at their own window, eh, Maise?' I said. 'It's quite possible you could have made a mistake!'

Maise came right up to me and put her face an inch away from mine. 'Now, listen here, Martin King, I'm just glad my Kevin wasn't with you while you were performing lurid sex acts with girls. You don't know where and who they've been with. Just think of the diseases you could be spreading! And God forbid you ever put one of these girls in the family way!' As a parting shot, she said, 'Wait till I tell your mother!' She held out her hand: 'And I want your front-door key.'

I placed it in her palm and she dropped it into her purse.

'Me and your mum knew you were up to something! I'm just glad my little Kevin isn't involved.'

'No,' I thought to myself, 'your precious little virgin Kevin is going to get a kick right up the bollocks, because your little fucking Kevin was meant to be my look-out!'

'Right, out you go,' said Maise, escorting me down the stairs.

When I looked across the square, my number-one security guard was involved in a game of five-a-side football and hadn't even noticed his mother's return.

Kevin finished his game and strolled over, unaware of what had

gone on. As far as he knew, I'd just finished riding the arse off Susie.
'All right, Mart?' he said. 'Where's your chick gone?'

I gave him an icy glare. 'I thought I asked you to keep dog.'

'I did,' he said, 'but I must have got distracted by the game of football.'

'So you didn't see your mum heading my way, then?'

'No,' he said, 'obviously not. What did she say to you?'

'Not a lot, really,' I told him, 'just that she's glad that you weren't with me.'

'What about Sue? Did my mum catch you with her?'

'Nearly,' I said, 'and she's taken our front-door key away.'

'More importantly, did you give Sue a good seeing-to?'

'I would've done, Kev, if you'd been doing your job properly.'

'Sorry, Mart,' he said. 'It won't happen again.'

We met up with the girls later at the disco and had a last slow dance with them. The night ended and we arranged to see them at the reception at ten o'clock the following morning.

We all turned up to say our goodbyes and there were plenty of tears from the girls even though we'd agreed to meet up in a couple of weeks' time.

Steve, a West Ham fan we'd been knocking about with all week, said he wanted to come along when we went up to north London to see the girls. He lived in Hackney, which wasn't too far away, and he said he would look forward to seeing us all again. We'd made some good friends that week.

A few weeks later we made the trip up to Edmonton in north London to see Sue and Jill. Steve turned up with a few of his pals and we all went for a Wimpy. The talk soon got round to football and fashion. Steve unbuttoned his Crombie and showed off his new trousers. They were like a Rupert the Bear check. And he wore a pair of brown fringe-and-buckle loafers. He did look the business.

'Where did you get the strides, then, Steve?' I asked hardly able to contain my excitement at the prospect of being the first of my lot to own something new on the fashion scene.

'There's a menswear shop right opposite the station at Liverpool Street. Because the shop's near Petticoat Lane market, it's even open on a Sunday morning,' he told me.

My mind was made up and when I got home that evening I asked Dad to call me at six o'clock the next morning. I told him I was going on a mission.

'But you don't normally get up that early,' said Dad, trying to work out what I was up to. The trouble with parents is that they always seem to be able to suss you out when you're up to something, no matter how innocent it is.

'I know,' I reassured him, 'but I want to get my paper round done early so that I can get up to London and do some shopping!'

'What, on a Sunday?' snorted the old man, still thinking I wasn't telling the truth.

Next day I was the first paper-boy to arrive at Ginger's. The man who owned the corner shop rubbed his eyes in disbelief. 'I must be dreaming,' he said. 'You're normally the last one here, not the first.'

'I might be the last one here every day, but I'm always the first one back.'

Ginger nodded. I nipped round with the papers and was back within half an hour. I ran the couple of miles to Colliers Wood Station and caught the tube up to Liverpool Street. The city streets, which on weekdays were filled with office workers, were deserted. I looked up at the big clock above the station. Seven thirty, it said.

A tramp asked me for money. 'Spare some change for a cup of tea, son?'

I noticed he had two black eyes – must have upset someone when he was begging. He shouldn't have been worrying about cups of tea – he should have invested any money ponced in karate lessons.

I found the shop I was looking for and scanned the window for the check trousers. I couldn't see them and panic set in – all this way for fuck all! I stepped back to look at the name above the shop. It was definitely the right place. Where were the fucking trousers? I noticed a smaller window round the side of the shop and in it to my relief were the strides. Now I just had to hope they had them in my size. 'If they haven't,' I thought, 'I'll squeeze into a size smaller, or wear a belt with something bigger. Either way, I'm not going home empty-handed.'

The list of opening times hung from the glass door: 'OPEN SUNDAYS 10 a.m. – 3 p.m.' I glanced back up at the clock. Seven forty, it read. Shit, nearly another two and a half hours to waste!

I decided to have a walk around Petticoat Lane which even at this time of day was already buzzing, mostly, it seemed, with foreign tourists. I passed the stall where Dad had bought my Crombie over-coat. The little bald Jewish fella was rushing around helping customers to get the heavy coats on and off. I stopped and listened to him. Yeah, it was the same patter he gave Dad when we were buying my coat: 'Looks lovely, sir', 'Fits like a glove', 'It's a bit big, but you'll soon grow into it'. I laughed and walked on.

The old boy who followed all the England games dressed in a Union Jack top hat and red tailcoat was busy setting up his stall. He sold football scarves, posters and pennants, all of which must have helped finance his trips around the world to watch England play. He always seemed to be at the pitchside cheering the lads on, and the TV cameras always picked him out.

I passed the back streets filled with rubbish and left the sounds of the Lane behind me. Asian kids were playing outside the rundown blocks of flats where a large Jewish community had once lived. The rattle of sewing machines filled the air and the smell of spicy aromas made me feel hungry.

I came out onto Brick Lane. You could buy all sorts of bric-a-brac there, and there was an area called Club Row where you could purchase live animals – anything from dogs, cats, goats and budgies to chickens, parrots, ferrets and rats (free if you want to catch a local one). The RSPCA kept a close eye on what went on, and the market was always being threatened with closure.

There was a shoe shop in Brick Lane that was a right grotty little hole, but it was where you got the latest in skinhead fashion and they sold every type of Dr Martens. I looked in the window and could just about see the display through the filthy glass. The shop never had a light on, so it always looked like the place was in semi-darkness. 'NEW IN' one label said, and below were a pair of oxblood-red Dr Marten shoes, priced £3. Alongside them were slip-on loafers with or without tassels, brogues, smooths, box Gibsons and wet-look Gibsons. I went inside. The place was packed. Skins from all over London and beyond were busily trying on shoes. The old Jew boy who owned the shop was up and down the wooden steps with boxes of shoes that were stacked high on shelves. His wife stood at the till, taking the money. The place was a gold-mine. There were people in every corner of the shop, sitting and standing as they tried on boots and shoes.

'Who's next?' asked the man, and within seconds he was back up his little ladder. I noticed a few West Ham fans with their claret-and-blue scarves on waiting to be served. A skin with a Spurs scarf came in but soon left when the West Ham fans gave him some eyeball. I never wore colours when I came up to east London. It was a predominantly West Ham area so you'd have to be mad to wear a Chelsea scarf up there – that was just asking for trouble.

I decided to head back down to the shop at Liverpool Street. As I passed through Club Row I noticed an Asian man leading a billy goat on a piece of string down the middle of the road. People were steering clear of the goat's huge horns.

I got back to the clothes shop just as they were opening up. I was their first customer of the day. I just hoped they had what I wanted, and in my size. Fingers crossed.

'How can I help you, sir?' asked the man serving, as he gave me the once-over.

'Sir!' I thought. 'Is he taking the piss? I'm only a kid – how can I be a sir?'

'I'd like a pair of those Rupert the Bear check trousers you have in the window,' I told him.

'Certainly, sir,' he said. 'What size would sir like?' He was getting right on my nerves.

'Twenty-eight waist, please.'

'Certainly, sir, I'll just get you a pair,' and he came back moments later with my size. 'Would sir like to try them on?'

'No, just bung them in a bag and sir will take them home, where sir's mum will make any alterations necessary,' I said. I handed over the money, threw the receipt in the bag and headed for home well pleased with myself.

As soon as I got back, I went straight upstairs and tried on the new trousers. They were a perfect fit. I put on my white socks and maroon fringe-and-buckle loafers topped off with a navy-blue Fred Perry. I looked the bollocks.

As I came down the stairs, Mum was waiting at the bottom and even she agreed how smart I looked. 'Very nice,' she said without a hint of piss-taking in her voice. 'All your mates have already been round this morning wanting to know where you are. "You tell me," I said to them. "He got up early this morning and he's off out some-where." Dinner will be ready at two!' she went on, but I was no longer listening as I ran up the road to the park.

I slowed down as I reached the gates and gave myself the once-over. I felt good because I knew no one around this area had trousers anything like these ones, plus the boys would have been wondering where I'd been today. I walked through the gates and a few of the lads were lazing about on the grass after a game of football. I strolled towards them and I could see them all staring. Not one of them said a word.

'All right, boys?' I said and could see all eyes were on my trousers. I sat down.

'We came around your house this morning,' said Tony, 'but you were out.' He couldn't take his eyes off the strides.

'Come on, you jealous bastards, say something,' I thought.

'Yeah, Mum told me,' I said.

This went on for ages with no mention of where I'd been, or had I bought some new trousers. They were jealous and it showed. 'I'll just wait for the time when they get something new and I'll give them a dose of their own medicine,' I told myself.

A couple of days later I talked to Sue on the phone and she told me she'd spoken to Steve from Hackney and that he'd asked her and Jill to come to the West Ham game at Stamford Bridge in a few days' time. We arranged to meet outside the Rising Sun pub, just opposite the Shed entrance to the ground, at about half past one.

'Okay,' I said, 'I'll look forward to seeing you there. Before you go,' I added, 'I bought a pair of those check trousers Steve had on.'

'Oh really,' she said, but I could tell by her voice she wasn't at all interested.

'Jealous cow!' I said to myself as I put the phone down, 'you're just like my mates.'

On the day of the match the gang I went with were meeting at Wimbledon Station at midday. It was safety in numbers when you played West Ham, even at Stamford Bridge. You all had to stick together when you played them. Every year they would come into the Shed end of the ground, thousands of them. They'd get to the ground early and stand on the home supporters' end. All they had to do was hide their claret-and-blue scarves and, once inside, they'd chase the Chelsea fans out from under the Shed and make it their end for the day.

We arrived at Fulham Broadway but before going out onto the street we took off our blue-and-white colours and hid them in our coats or round our waists out of sight. The street leading to the ground was full of West Ham fans and a Chelsea boy walking next to me was punched in the face and his rosette ripped from his jacket.

'Fucking hell, that could have been me,' I thought.

The West Ham bloke and his mates walked off laughing, kicking the Chelsea rosette along the ground.

Our mob split up immediately. What happened to 'we must stick together'? I was on my own. 'What should I do?' I wondered. 'Shall I go back home on the train and tell the others that I lost my money?' Seeing that bloke getting punched had really unnerved me. I kept walking. A group of West Ham skins were leaning up against the wall of the pub. Shit, this was where I was meant to meet Sue. I looked about but I didn't want to catch anyone's eye. A bloke with a Chelsea bobble-hat on got kicked up the arse by one of the West Ham lot and they threw his hat to the ground, shrieking with laughter. The West Ham mob mimicked how the bloke tried to cling to his hat. 'You wouldn't dare do that to Eccles,' I was thinking.

'Fucking doughnuts!' said a big West Ham skin as he whipped the hat from another unsuspecting bloke's head.

I'd seen enough. I crossed the road to join the queue to get in. Once inside, though, it was wall-to-wall West Ham. They were everywhere, all under the cover of the Shed. I pushed through the crowd and stood outside the tea bar at the back of the Shed, near the Bovril entrance. I noticed a few familiar Chelsea faces and listened in to what was being said by two blokes talking about the annual West Ham invasion. I kept quiet and stood alongside them, leaning on one of the barriers. 'It's fucking out of order,' one of them said, almost whispering and nervously looking around as if he knew he could be attacked at any minute.

His mate agreed as they both clapped the teams out onto the pitch. The Chelsea players ran towards the Shed end only to be met by boos and jeers from the West Ham fans packed behind the goal. Normally they were greeted by Chelsea fans singing their names. The looks on the players' faces said it all – they couldn't work out what was going on.

'*Chelsea! Chelsea!*' sang the fifty or so home fans standing around me. A few West Ham fans pushed towards us. A Chelsea bloke in his mid-twenties threw a right hook which landed on the temple of a tall skinhead with a West Ham scarf around his neck. The victim stumbled but grabbed the metal crush barrier to stop himself landing on the concrete terrace. This halted the West Ham mob in their tracks. A twenty-foot gap opened up and I ducked under the crush barrier out of the way. A few Chelsea boys melted into the crowd, but the fella who threw the punch stood his ground.

'Mind your backs, lads!' shouted a voice from behind but it was too late as a West Ham mob attacked us from the rear. Vicious fighting broke out all around, so I ducked back under the crush barrier. The West Ham boys who were standing under the cover of the Shed rushed towards us. We were surrounded but the cavalry arrived in the shape of the boys in blue and they managed to push the West Ham fans back. I felt a bit safer now that the Old Bill were there to keep an eye on things. I even had time to watch the game.

Suddenly, to my surprise, I heard someone calling my name from the West Ham side of the Old Bill. Sue, Jill and Steve were waving to me. 'Come over here!' yelled Steve.

'You're fucking joking!' I shouted back. 'I ain't that fucking mad!'

'Mind your language,' said a burly copper, 'or you'll be out.'

A big West Ham skinhead gave me daggers and drew his fingers across his throat. I ignored him. 'I got my trousers,' I shouted to Steve lifting one leg to show him. He gave me the thumbs-up.

'Why don't you go and stand over there with your boyfriend?' smirked the copper. I didn't reply, the sarcastic bastard.

West Ham scored and their fans went berserk. The Chelsea supporters made a half-hearted attempt to push towards their mob, but no one really wanted to get at them. Then I spotted Steve celebrating the goal. He had his arms around Sue and was giving her a full-blown passionate kiss on the lips. His tongue was halfway down her throat and she wasn't exactly trying too hard to stop him. From where I stood she looked like she was enjoying it. He was even thrusting his hips into her, and she was rubbing the back of his hair.

'Fucking bitch!' I muttered. I'd seen enough of this live sex show and, with little over fifteen minutes to go before the end of the game, I headed for the exit. Them two could go fuck themselves.

My team had lost, and I'd lost my bird. What a fucking day. Worse still, I'd got these silly fucking check trousers on. I hated them, women and football, in that order.

TWELVE

Stoke City

Chelsea's next appearance at Wembley after the glorious Cup final win over Leeds United was against Stoke City in the League Cup final. The League Cup wasn't as glamorous as the FA Cup, but a day out at Wembley was worth looking forward to. I'd been up to Stoke's ground a few years previously and was impressed by the passion shown by the Stoke fans. The Victoria Ground where they played was a compact stadium and their fans really got behind the team. Like most teams up north, though, the supporters rarely travelled down to London *en masse*. Manchester United were the exception to that rule, of course, but I'd seen Everton, Forest and Leeds all having a go at taking the Shed with little success.

I'd gone up to Stoke for a league game with a few of the lads from Tooting. After our trip to Leeds, word soon got around about how well we'd done up there, so a few more people were beginning to travel to away games. Today's British Rail football special was packed with Chelsea boys heading to the Stoke match and the talk on the train was that the home support's end of the ground was where we should all meet. We didn't know much about the Stoke fans. Our Arsenal, West Ham and Spurs mates had never spoken about going in the Stoke end of the ground, so we would be treading new ground if we did it today. I listened to a couple of the older blokes talking about how they'd been up to the Victoria Ground before and how game the Stoke boys were. 'They will be right up for it,' one said, 'and if we do go in their end, expect a real fight, because believe us they're no mugs. After the game up there last time, we came out of the ground and their boys were out on the streets waiting for us. The funny thing is, they were a bit wary of our reputation, so they didn't come straight into the Chelsea mob. That gave us time to all get out of the ground and face up to them. Someone threw a bottle from our side which landed right in the middle of them, and it caused a bit of panic. The Old Bill moved in and split up the two mobs and we walked side by side back to the railway station. If it weren't for the Old Bill with dogs and horses keeping the two mobs apart, God knows what would have happened. Try and stick together because I'm sure they'll be waiting somewhere between the station and the ground.'

I'd more than a few away games under my belt and saw myself as an old hand. I didn't feel nervous, just excited, with a sense of not knowing what was going to happen.

On arriving at Stoke Station we were met by lines of coppers all along the platform. There had been a lot of publicity in the press and on TV about skinheads and steel-toecapped boots. The press had dubbed them 'Bovver Boots' and there were calls for the Home Secretary to ban the wearers from football grounds. There had even been a documentary on TV using a tailor's dummy to illustrate the damage that a kick from a steel-toecapped boot could inflict. 'Look at that, boy!' the old man had said as we sat watching this garbage. The presenter had slipped on a commando boot and kicked the dummy in the head. Bits of pink plastic went everywhere as the head shattered. It wasn't even realistic. 'You ain't wearing yours no more, that's it! You won't be seeing those boots of yours again!'

I sat there and laughed. I thought the telly was meant to be a bad influence on the kids, not on the parents, but my lot believed everything they watched.

'In the morning, Fred,' Mum said to Dad, 'you throw them boots on the fire and burn them!'

'Actually, Mum,' I interrupted, 'they're three sizes too big and they don't belong to me – they're Alan's old work boots!'

The Old Bill lined us up along the platform and tested to see if we were wearing steel-toecaps by treading on the toes of our boots.

Some fucking great big aggressive bastard who weighed about twenty stone shifted his weight on to one leg and pressed his foot down on my toes. 'You fucking wanker!' I thought, as he stood in front of me and grinned. I limped off out into the street.

'Next!' he shouted.

'He could have broken your toes,' said Jeff, laughing. 'He only had to bend down and squeeze your toecaps with his fingers.'

'He couldn't do that,' I grumbled, 'that fucking great belly he had hanging over his trousers would have made it impossible for him to bend over.'

We waited for everyone to get together and then we headed off towards the ground, boot inspection complete. There were about five hundred of us and everyone kept together. The police led the way and brought up the rear with a few on horseback and a couple of dog handlers. It was less than an hour to kick-off so we were expecting a warm welcome from the Stoke fans. At every crossroads we came to the mob almost ground to a halt. 'Keep moving!' yelled the Old Bill. We saw the odd one or two Stoke fans, but when they spotted us coming they disappeared up a side street or into a shop. A few locals stood on their doorsteps and watched the Chelsea boys walk silently past. As we got nearer the ground there were more fans milling about. We saw some Chelsea fans queuing for the away supporters' end. That's where we should have queued, but instead we carried on up the road and joined the queue for the Stoke end. We got some strange looks from the local fans already there but no one said a word. We seemed to have lost our police escort and there were no coppers to be seen at the turnstiles. We paid our money to the man on the gate and he clicked the turnstile and let us through one at a time. We could hear the Stoke fans inside chanting their team's name.

We followed the rest of the Chelsea fans out onto the large covered terrace. It was jam-packed. We pushed our way through the crowds and stood at the back, behind the goal. Stoke fans around us ducked out of our way and moved to behind the crush barriers. I doubted the police knew we'd infiltrated the home end. They were probably none the wiser to what was going on. There must have been around two hundred of us in this end and I could tell the Stoke boys were getting a bit upset. They started to gather round us, giving it plenty of verbal, but for the time being they didn't come too close.

'*Zigger Zagger, Zigger Zagger!*' chanted a voice within the Stoke fans.

'*Oi Oi Oi!*' the rest of them roared back.

'*Zigger Zagger, Zigger Zagger!*' he chanted again in a deep rasping voice.

'*Oi Oi Oi!*' the others repeated.

We all looked at one another in disbelief. Those thieving Stoke bastards had nicked the chant that was synonymous with us Chelsea fans! It was a bit like The Beatles nicking a song off The Rolling Stones. Mick Greenaway, one of the originators of the Shed at Chelsea, was said to have started that chant down at the Bridge, and he did it with more style and panache than this bastard could manage. The Chelsea fans replied with a rendition of 'Maybe it's because I'm a Londoner' and the Stoke fans tried to drown us out with hissing and booing. That was the signal for a ruck to break out. As we scattered the Stoke fans down the terraces, our boys at the opposite end came to life, roaring out '*Chelsea! Chelsea!*' from the terrace where the bulk of the Chelsea fans were gathered. They could see us taking the Stoke end and were giving us a bit of vocal support.

The fighting was over within a minute and the police surrounded us. The Stoke fans, safe in the knowledge that we were penned in by the Old Bill, returned to where they had been standing before Chelsea embarrassingly ran them. 'City! City!' they chanted, and the sound echoed around under the massive roof.

There were a few more skirmishes but nothing major and the game ended with the police holding us back and then escorting us back to the train station. I was disappointed by the lack of Stoke fans out on the streets afterwards. The walk back to the train was relatively quiet and all in all it felt like a feather in the cap for the Chelsea Shed boys. The taking of the Stoke end would look good on our CV.

I had nothing but admiration for the Stoke City fans after that day's game and from then on I used to look out for their results in the

Sunday papers. It's funny how just one visit to a ground could change your perception of that club. With Stoke I think it was the passion the fans had for their team that surprised me. They'd never won anything, yet the fans were right behind them. All that good feeling was to change, though, when Chelsea and Stoke City met at Wembley for the League Cup final.

After the nightmare queue for tickets for the Watford game in the FA Cup semi-final, we promised ourselves we would make some money next time Chelsea were selling tickets for a big game. Everything was in place the day before the tickets went on sale at Stamford Bridge – until, that is, I discovered my dad had left his flask at work, so the tea-selling business was out of the window. Tony's brother had taken his camping stove away on a fishing trip, so no eggs and bacon for the hungry queue either, and Ginger in the paper shop wouldn't entertain the idea of us buying the Sunday papers in bulk. 'Twenty papers isn't what I call bulk,' he said. So, in the end, we didn't even bother going over to the Bridge on the morning the tickets went on sale. Instead, we had the idea that if we went to Wembley Stadium early on the morning of the final, we could bunk in over the fence. We'd seen people on the telly doing it, so we'd give it a go. We had no tickets, so what did we have to lose?

I didn't think much of the idea. 'Let's go a month early and tunnel our way in,' I said sarcastically. Tony and Jeff weren't amused. I knew we had no chance of climbing in, but the other two wouldn't listen. On the morning of the day of the game we were over at Wembley by nine o'clock and to our surprise we saw that some other daft fuckers had had the same idea. We walked round and round the stadium looking for a way in, but every entrance and exit was bristling with burly security guards. We had no chance. After a couple of hours of walking aimlessly around, we sat on a wall at the top of Wembley Way and asked everyone who passed if they had any spare tickets. 'Sorry, boys,' was the usual answer.

We were just about to give up when we got talking to Dave, a ginger-haired Chelsea fan in his late teens. I'd seen him in the Shed a couple of times. He told us he was going to mug a Stoke fan and nick their tickets and swap them with a tout for a ticket in the Chelsea end.

'Come on,' he said, 'why don't you and your mates do it with me?'

Jeff, Tony and I looked at one another. 'We've got nothing to lose,' said Jeff and we jumped down off the wall and followed Dave out into the vast Wembley carpark. A few of the other Chelsea lads desperate for tickets had overheard the conversation and tagged along.

'Here we go!' said Dave, as a coach full of Stoke City fans drove past us and parked. We walked towards the coach and stopped about twenty yards away. 'Right, duck down behind these parked cars,' said Dave. 'The plan is when they get near us, we jump out on them and I put my hand inside my Crombie and make out I've got a knife. They shit themselves and hand over their tickets. We then all fuck off and meet back up at the top of Wembley Way. Understood?'

We all nodded. I watched the first of the Stoke fans heading our way, threading their way through the hundreds of parked cars. A couple of blokes who looked in their late twenties led the way as the rest of the coach emptied out behind them. They had red-and-white straw boaters on their heads and great big red Stoke City rosettes pinned to their chests. When they stumbled upon us, Dave jumped up and stuck his hand in his coat pocket. The blokes couldn't work out what was going on.

'I've got a fucking great commando knife here!' growled Dave. 'And if you don't hand over your match tickets I'm going to cut you wide open!'

Whack! One of the blokes punched Dave straight on the jaw and he was out cold before he even hit the deck. His head smacked against the ground. I'd seen enough and took to my heels. The rest of the coach party, seeing what was going on, gave chase. 'Stop them!' they shouted.

Out of the corner of my eye I saw Jeff dive under a parked car and try to hide himself. I'd seen him do that many a time playing hide and seek when we were kids. He was a master of getting away. Tony headed off in the opposite direction to me and seemed to have no one chasing him. I reached the top of Wembley Way and luckily there were thousands of people now walking around. I joined a queue for hotdogs and noticed the Stoke fans stop and look around for me.

'We've lost him,' I heard one of them say. They would have been better off keeping quiet now, and they knew it. There were thousands of Chelsea fans outside the stadium, so they wouldn't have fared too well if they had caught me and given me a slap. One of them spotted me. He nudged his mate and they both stared at me, not quite sure if I was the one they were looking for.

Some Chelsea boys noticed the red and white of Stoke in amongst them and started crowding around these two northerners. 'Well, well, boys, look what we've got here,' I heard one big Chelsea fan say to his mates.

As soon as my pursuers were distracted I was off like a shot. I ran against the flow of people and headed for the tube station. Standing outside was Tony. 'Where's Jeff?' he asked.

'Fuck knows,' I replied. 'I saw him dive under a car. He'll probably wait till it gets dark or the owner comes back, and then he'll make his way home.'

We decided it was too risky to hang around, so we headed off towards home. Tony suggested we go and see how his brother was getting on fishing over at Mitcham Common. I hated fishing – I found it so boring – but there was fuck all else to do. When we got over to the One Island pond we found his brother fast asleep in his one-man nylon tent. We were halfway through his sandwiches and flask before he woke up. Why people raved about fishing I could never understand. No wonder his brother fell asleep. There can't be that many sports where you can fall asleep and still claim to be enjoying yourself. Fishing and darts! The mind boggled at those two activities being called a sport – you were hardly likely to break out in a sweat doing either. I left Tony at the end of my road just as my brother appeared round the corner, clutching an evening paper with the football results inside.

'Your team done well, boy,' he said.

'Why, what was the score?' I asked excitedly, trying to grab the paper from him.

'Chelsea lost two goals to one.'

'You liar!' I grabbed the paper and there, in black and white, was the score.

I couldn't believe it. The entire day had been one big fuck-up. The sound of *Zigger Zagger, Zigger Zagger!* came into my head, but it wasn't Greenaway.

THIRTEEN

Play Up, Pompey

I had been playing football on a sunny Friday afternoon after school and a dozen or so of the boys and I were sitting around wondering what to do with ourselves that evening. There were no local dances or discos on and we were bored shitless.

'How about going over to the youth club at Pollards Hill,' someone suggested. No one seconded that, so that idea went out of the window.

'Let's catch the train to Hampton Court and dive off the bridge and have a swim in the Thames,' said someone else. It wasn't a bad idea but we knew by the time we got there the sun would have gone down and it wouldn't be warm enough for swimming. No, give that a miss. It would take us a couple of hours to get over there on the bus and train anyway.

'How about the pictures?' suggested Peter.

'What's on?' we asked him.

'Christopher Lee in *The Brides of Dracula*,' he answered in a voice just above a whisper, making an effort to scare the younger ones among us. It certainly had the desired effect. Every one of us went quiet. Just the mention of a Hammer House film sent shivers down our spines. They were the ultimate in horror films.

'Fuck that!' a few lads said.

'Anyway, it's an X-rated film and none of us look over eighteen, so we'd never get in – much as we'd love to go,' I lied.

'You don't know unless you try!' said Peter. 'Come on, what have you got to lose? It'll be a laugh. The lot of us have never been to the pictures together.'

I knew I wouldn't be laughing, that was for sure. There was a programme on TV called *The Invisible Man* and it scared the life out of me – and it was only about a man who was supposed to be invisible. All you saw were some bandages and a hat floating about. When it came on I used to hide my face behind a pillow and jump on Dad's lap. I knew I'd probably shit myself in the darkness of the cinema if Christopher Lee showed us his bloodstained gnashers.

Suddenly, though, all the others thought it was a great idea. 'Yeah, let's all go!' a few of them said.

I wasn't too sure but I didn't want to lose face. It annoyed me, though: why should I fork out good money for something I knew I wasn't going to enjoy? It was the same as eating a meal you knew would make you throw up – I could see no sense in it. But how was I going to get out of this?

'The film's showing at the Odeon at Tooting Broadway,' said Peter, 'so let's all meet outside the pictures at seven.' Everyone agreed.

How many times had I seen this lot agree to go to football and then fail to turn up, I wondered. Too numerous to mention. That was good enough for me. 'Fuck them,' I thought. 'I ain't going, and that's that, but I won't tell them. I just won't turn up.' I jumped to my feet, picked up my jumper that had been acting as a goalpost, tied it round my waist and told everyone I'd catch them later.

As I walked home, I started to think about the Dracula film. Why should I pay good money to go and have the shit scared out of me? I walked through the front door and straight away, just from the look on my face, Mum knew something was wrong. I suppose it was that motherly instinct that lets them know when something's wrong with their teenage babies.

'What's up, boy?' she asked. 'Have you seen a ghost?'

'No, it's nothing,' I lied as I slumped into the chair in front of the telly. She shrugged her shoulders and went back into the kitchen. The disgusting smell told me she must be preparing Dad's evening meal, or maybe someone had given her some meat for the dog.

'Want to try some of this?' she said, waving an empty packet under my nose. 'It's chicken and vegetables in a hot curry sauce. I thought I'd give it to your dad for a change. There's enough for two!'

'No thanks, Ma,' I said, 'but save some for Alan, he eats all that foreign muck.'

Dad came in and straight away asked what the awful smell was. 'I smelt it when I turned the corner at the top of the road,' he announced. 'It reminds me of Brick Lane on a Sunday morning.' It was only the other week he was moaning about getting sausage and mash every night for his dinner.

'I thought I'd give you a change, Fred, darling,' said Mum, 'You're always complaining that it's the same food every night, so I thought this would make a nice change from sausage.'

'Thanks all the same,' said Dad, trying not to hurt Mum's feelings, 'but I was a bit peckish dinner time at work, so I had a roast dinner in the works canteen and now I don't feel that hungry. Perhaps Alan will have it, he likes that exotic stuff.'

I glanced at Dad. 'Roast dinner at dinner time!' I said to him and he glared at me, shook his fist as if to say 'be quiet' and then laughed as the doorbell rang and Mum went to answer it.

She stopped to check her hair in the hall mirror before opening the door. 'I wonder who this could be,' we heard her ask herself, changing the tone of her voice in readiness to greet who ever it might be. One second she was plain old Mrs King, the jolly cockney, the next she was Lady Penelope Braithwaite-Brown, second cousin twice removed to Her Majesty the Queen. The transformation was unbelievable.

'Well, open the bleedin' door and find out,' shouted Dad, and we both laughed.

'Come in,' we heard her say and then ask whoever it was if their mother was all right. 'Mart,' she called, 'it's Peter.'

Shit! He's come round for me to go to the pictures. Shall I make out I'm asleep? No, they'll only wake me up. Shall I tell him I've got the flu? No, that won't work either — I saw him only an hour ago. I know, I'll tell him I'm skint and can't afford to go, and I've got to go with Mum and Dad to visit my nan. Then it'll soon be byebye, Peter.

'All right, Pete,' I said.

He sat down beside me. 'Ain't you ready yet, Kingy?'

'No, no,' I said, 'I'm afraid I won't be coming.'

'Why's that?' he asked.

'I'm skint, I ain't got a pot to piss in.'

The old man shot me a look. 'Don't use that expression, boy!' he said.

'Sorry, Dad,' I said. I turned to Peter. 'I'd love to go to the pictures but I just can't afford it. Tell the rest of the boys I'm sorry, but I didn't realise just how skint I was.'

'I'll lend you the money till next week,' said Peter, 'I'm flush. My dad gave me a tip for a greyhound, a rank outsider, which came in at ten to one. And I had two quid on it to win, so have a couple of pounds, and weigh me in when you've got it.'

'Just fuck off!' I thought to myself. 'I don't want to go to the stupid fucking pictures! Can't you get it into your thick fucking head! I don't want to go!'

Dad interrupted my thoughts and pulled some coins from his pocket, throwing them into my lap. 'Go on, boy, don't let your mate down. Go with him. You can count your real friends on one hand. It's nice of your mate to offer to pay for you.'

Pete grinned. He knew I didn't fancy it, but thanks to Dad it looked like I was going anyway.

'I'll just go and get changed,' I muttered and off I went upstairs to my room. Suddenly a flash of inspiration hit me. I knew if I went into the toilet and stuck my fingers down my throat I could force myself to puke up. I'd call Mum and tell her to tell Peter that I'd come over bad and that I couldn't go with him. Brilliant idea! I went into the bathroom and lifted up the toilet seat and knelt down on the floor. I positioned my head over the kazi and was just about to start when I was suddenly lifted up from behind. It was my brother, Alan, telling me to go and wash my hair somewhere else, as he was about to get in the bath. He dumped me on my bed and I heard him slam and lock the bathroom door. 'Fucking wanker!' I shouted back at him. I got changed and reluctantly went off to the pictures, thanks to my helpful family.

'Didn't you want to go?' asked Peter as we walked towards the bus-stop. I could see some of the others were already waiting.

'Fucking hell, they're keen,' I muttered under my breath. I looked at Peter. 'What gave you the idea I didn't want to go?' I asked aloud. 'I wouldn't miss this for the world.'

The bus arrived and we all dashed upstairs. Everyone sat at the back. 'Where are Fred and Tass?' I asked.

'They're meeting us there,' someone said.

I sat back and looked out the window. It didn't seem that long ago that our lot used to go to the Saturday-morning pictures together. Those were the days – sixpence to get in and three hours of non-stop old black-and-white films. There would be a sing-song before the films started, with every kid joining in. The favourite was 'A Spoonful of Sugar Helps the Medicine Go Down'. A little white dot on the screen followed underneath the words to the song, as we sung our hearts out. Kids would chuck things at the man playing the giant organ in the orchestra pit. When you came out at midday after the show there would be a mad rush for the baker's next door where you could get little jam buns for one penny each. We'd spend our bus-fare home on more buns, and then walk back with our bellies full up all the way to Mitcham. Those were handsome times.

When we jumped off the bus tonight, right outside the picture-house, I saw Tass and Fred waiting. Fred had his back to me and when he turned round, I pissed myself laughing when I noticed the stick-on sideburns he was wearing. Fred was only about four foot tall so with these black hairy things hanging from his cheeks he looked like a midget version of Elvis Presley. Tass was trying to smoke a fag but not inhale and he was going a funny grey colour. He wasn't a smoker. The pair of them were trying their hardest to look and act older, when in fact all they were doing was making themselves out to be a right pair of planks.

To my surprise, everyone who said they were coming had turned up. We filed into the foyer and Peter, the eldest among us, paid his money to the woman in the glass booth. She issued him with a pink ticket which the man in a suit and dickie-bow standing next to the booth ripped in half, handing Peter back part of the ticket. I went next and I didn't get a second look. I'd made it! I handed the ticket to Mr Dickhead, who gave me my half of it back. Tass was next. He was well over six foot tall, so even without the dog-end hanging from his lips he'd have had no trouble getting in. Then it was Fred's turn. The woman looked at him, then looked at the man, who looked back at her and the pair of them burst out laughing. The woman handed Fred his ticket and off he trotted to buy some popcorn. He grinned at me and Peter as if to say 'I made it'.

'Excuse me, sir, not so quick,' said the man to Fred. Fred froze to the spot, his jubilation short lived. 'Can I clip your ticket?' and the man handed Fred his torn ticket.

The rest of us got in too and we were shown to our seats by a man shining a torch in the darkness. We all sat in the front row and settled back to watch the main feature. First, though, there was a short film about a tribe in Africa who didn't seem to wear any clothes. Every time a woman came on with her tits hanging out there were fits of giggles and stifled laughter. Next were the adverts, including one telling you there was a decent Indian restaurant less than a hundred yards from this very cinema. 'You wouldn't catch me eating that shit,' said a bloke in a loud voice behind us.

The big red drape curtains closed then opened to reveal the screen with the title:

THE BRIDES OF DRACULA

The cinema went quiet. Nothing had even happened yet but I was already cacking my pants. I looked along the row and all of our lot were glued to the screen. Christopher Lee appeared and a few people in the audience booed and hissed. 'For fuck's sake, don't upset him!' I thought.

The story was mostly centred around a fog-filled graveyard and it wasn't long before Dracula had his first taste of blood. He laid out a right dollybird on a gravestone whose lungs are hanging out of her ripped dress, but instead of biting into her tits he goes for the neck.

I nudged Peter. 'You sure he ain't gay?'

After a while I realised there was nothing to be scared of and that the film was really quite tame. After about three-quarters of an hour the lights came on and a voice over the tannoy said there would be a short intermission. The others rushed off to join the queue for ice-cream. 'Shall we fuck off?' Peter said to me. 'This is bollocks.'

Half of us wanted to stay and the other half wanted to go. 'I don't want to hang around,' said Peter, 'only I'm going to football in the morning to see Millwall play down at Portsmouth.' Without thinking, I told him to count me in. 'Count you in!' he said. 'Chelsea's your team – why would you want to go to Pompey with Millwall?'

'To see the rows,' I replied. There had always been aggro between the two teams.

'Right,' he shrugged. 'Be round my house at seven thirty in the morning and I'll take you to meet all my Millwall mates.'

'You're on,' I told him.

I hardly slept a wink that night as I tossed and turned with excitement. Eventually I fell asleep, but I was up and out the house at six to do my paper round. Ginger paid me my wages for the week and I hurried round to Peter's. After five minutes of banging on the front door, he opened it up, still in his jim-jams. I had him down as the playboy type, someone who slept in the nude. I bet he still had a favourite teddy bear.

'Nice pyjamas, Pete,' I told him.

He was embarrassed that I knew what he wore in bed. 'What time is it, Kingy?' he said, rubbing the sleep out of his eyes.

'Seven o'clock,' I said, 'so get your skates on!'

Two minutes later he was dressed and we were out of the house, walking up the road sharing a packet of Custard Creams he'd taken from his kitchen cupboard. We took a bus to Kennington and cut through the back streets to East Lane, where the stall-holders of the street market were getting their pitches ready for the normal Saturday rush. My mum used to bring me down here when I was a young kid and later on I'd come shopping here with my mates. There was a blinding shop called Fox's that sold all the latest skinhead gear. We walked the length of the market, with Peter waving and nodding to people who were asking him what today's result would be. He was well known in the area and it made me feel good, being with some-one who was a bit of a face.

'I used to hang around this market all the time,' he told me. 'I used to bunk off school and come down here and help out the stall-holders. They'd bung me a few quid. In the end I didn't bother going to school and I got in so much trouble the family decided to move from Peckham down to where we now live in Mitcham.'

A group of youths about twenty-strong emerged from a tower block in the centre of the estate we were walking through. Peter stopped and chatted to them. 'You going today, Peter?' asked one of the boys as they shook hands.

'Yeah, I'm just going up to knock for Charlie. I'll get him out of bed, and then we're off to Waterloo to meet the rest of the chaps.'

'Save your legs!' said one of the boys, 'I saw Charlie leave about ten minutes ago with half a dozen other fellas. They looked like they'd had a heavy night. They were moaning the lifts weren't working and that they'd had to walk down twenty flights of stairs.'

I looked up at the tower block they were talking about, puzzled. Who planned this type of housing, people all stacked and living on top of one another?

Peter was annoyed that Charlie and his mates had fucked off with-out him. 'I told him I'd be here early and the wanker still didn't wait! Martin and me will come with you lot,' he said, introducing me to all of them, even telling them I was a Shed boy.

We walked back up the Old Kent Road, where we jumped on a bus to Waterloo Station. When we got there Millwall fans were hanging about outside. Rumour had it that the old enemy, West Ham, were planning a surprise appearance before we left for Portsmouth.

When we got onto the concourse of the station, I couldn't believe my eyes. It was wall-to-wall Millwall and I was one of the youngest kids there. The myth surrounding the club – about the large dockers who followed them – certainly looked to be true. I'd never seen such big blokes. The Chelsea mob I was used to going with were mostly teenagers with a few older lads thrown in, but this Millwall mob had some real grizzly older blokes. Another rumour doing the rounds was that a train full of Millwall had already left for the south coast. The train we boarded was packed solid. It was a football special laid on by British Rail, so there was no buffet car. It was the normal run-of-the-mill old train supplied for football fans, but who could blame British Rail for providing old rolling stock when nearly every Saturday travelling supporters wrecked the trains carrying them to matches. This service was straight through to Portsmouth.

On arrival at Fratton Park, we were met by scores of police officers, many accompanied by Alsatians trying to stretch their leads an extra inch so they could take a chomp out of your arse. We piled out onto the street and stopped the traffic. This mob looked up for it.

'Keep to the footpath!' shouted a copper.

'Bollocks!' came back the reply, as half the mob crossed the road. Already the crowd had split in two and the Old Bill had lost control. Two hundred of us slipped up a side road and, to our surprise, when we looked behind us no Old Bill were following. We kept walking, heading, it seemed, away from the ground. We saw a pub up ahead of us, but having a drink was the last thing on this mob's mind. A crowd appeared in front of us, quickly joined by reinforcements from the pub, many of whom were armed with glasses and bottles. I saw one man waving a snooker cue above his head. A shower of bottles started to rain down on us. The Millwall mob stopped in its tracks in front of the crowd from the pub, who were bouncing up and down. They seemed well game.

'Stand, Millwall, stand!' came a shout from the front. A wooden fence was ripped from a front garden and many of the Millwall boys armed themselves with pieces of timber. The bloke with the snooker cue ran into our front line and clocked a Millwall fan around the head with it and then sprinted off. We charged and the Pompey boys streamed back into the pub. The sound of glass smashing filled the street as the pub windows were put in. A Millwall fan picked up a wooden bench and threw it at four or five Pompey boys who were defending the front door from invasion. They gave that up as a lost cause as Millwall entered the pub. You wouldn't catch me going in there for love or money. Fifty or so Millwall boys decided to pursue the rest of the Pompey fans who had legged it up the road. I decided to stick with this lot. I hadn't a clue where Peter and his mates had gone but I felt safe with these blokes.

'Stick together, lads!' said a young Millwall warrior aged about forty. The rest of the mob, who by now had finished refurbishing the pub, caught us up.

'There's Old Bill everywhere,' I heard someone say, and sure enough behind us the street was filled with flashing blue lights. Coppers on foot ran up the road and grabbed the first person they could lay their hands on. I think it's called shutting the stable door after the horse has bolted or, in some people's book, random nicking.

After a while spent roaming around the back streets, we found ourselves back out on the main road that led to the ground. I saw Peter, who told me the two mobs had just clashed in the middle of the road. Groups of blokes were hanging around every street corner. The two mobs were, by the looks of it, intermingled with each other. I tried to stick as close as I could to Peter. I didn't want to let him out of my sight. He told me to follow a mob of Millwall that were on our right-hand side. The fifty or so geezers were Millwall's top boys, he informed me. We stopped at the corner of a street and this Millwall firm gathered round a small Pompey mob. Insults were exchanged. 'Come on, mugs, we're on your manor!' one of the Millwall mob said to the Pompey fans. They backed off and melted into the crowd.

The road led to the home supporters' end. Hundreds of fans were queuing to get in. The Millwall boys approached the three lines of Pompey fans shuffling towards the turnstiles who didn't realise they were about to get caught up in a full-scale punch-up. A few sensed something wasn't right and took off and hid their blue-and-white Pompey scarves. Others left the queue and walked away.

'Come on, boys, we're here,' growled a big Millwall fan in a size XXXL donkey jacket. He must have lost a Saturday-morning's over-time at the docks so he could come to this game. A Pompey fan told him to 'Fuck off up your own end' and was rewarded with a right-hander. The crowd backed off. The Millwall boys laughed at their cowardice but, to be fair, these guys didn't look like a football mob, though no doubt if they saw a Millwall fan lying on the ground, some of these blokes in the queue would put the boot in.

From around the corner came some Portsmouth fans chanting their team's name. They had no idea what was going on and stumbled across the Millwall firm. The two mobs faced one another in the middle of the street. Anyone who didn't fancy it got out of the way a bit sharpish. The Portsmouth boys were as game as the Millwall mob and the two groups clashed. The Pompey numbers were swelling as people, realising there was a ruck in progress, joined in. The Millwall boys were heavily outnumbered. I faded into the background and made out I was just queuing to get in. The Old Bill galloped up on horseback and quelled the disorder. They pushed the Millwall fans up the road towards the away fans' end of the ground and then blocked the road so I was stranded on the Pompey side. A few people gave me a look, like 'wasn't you with the Millwall mob a minute ago?' I put my head down and headed back out onto the main road. The Pompey fans were furious about what had gone on. Millwall had taken the piss. 'After the game it'll be different!' I heard one of them say. 'This time we'll be better organised. No way are those bastards going to take any more liberties!'

A few lone Millwall fans were savagely attacked by the Pompey mob, who were now intent on revenge. A group of Pompey fans were standing at the top of the road that led down to the Millwall end and were picking off Millwall fans just arriving. The Old Bill were fifty yards away and unaware of what was going on. I was on my own, so there was no way I was walking through that lot. There was only one thing for it – I'd have to stand in the Pompey end. I joined the queue and, once inside, stood at the back of the covered terrace. The home fans were expecting a Millwall invasion, so any new-comers were given the once over and treated with suspicion. I studied the programme I'd bought on the way in and just tried to not draw attention to myself. When the Pompey team was announced I clapped along with the rest of the crowd. The Millwall fans were packed tightly behind the goal at the far end of the ground. The police looked like they had their work cut out trying to keep them from getting onto the pitch. Every now and then the coppers would grab someone in the crowd and hurl them over the wall surroun-ding the pitch then frog-march them out of the ground. This went on all through the game and, at the final whistle, the police lines were finally breached as a few Millwall fans got onto the pitch, but there weren't enough of them to head in our direction.

I followed everyone out onto the street. The Old Bill moved on anyone standing around so I decided to head back to the station and catch the first train back to London. It seemed to stop at every station on the way back to the city, which was handy for me as I could get off at Wimbledon rather than go all the way back into Waterloo. I was surprised at just how many Pompey supporters travelled from the surrounding areas. They were still getting off the train as far north as Guildford.

When I reached Wimbledon I had to admit I'd enjoyed my day out with the Millwall lads. They certainly took their enthusiasm to a higher level than anything I'd ever witnessed at Chelsea, but in their own words: 'No one likes us, we don't care!' and I'd second that.

FOURTEEN

School's Out

It was the day after the borough sports day, when schools from all over the area had competed in track and field events. We were at morning assembly and our headmistress strode across the stage, stopped and faced the entire school. She normally had a face like thunder, but this morning before she'd even said a word you could tell she had the hump about something.

'Yesterday,' she said, 'members of this school were involved in a disgraceful incident with pupils from another school. Pupils from this school attacked other children and a bicycle was stolen. The boy who had his bicycle stolen was punched and kicked and friends of his were chased up the road, but managed to get away from the thugs who hurled foul and abusive language at them. I am ashamed to stand in front of you as headmistress of this school. The people involved should hang their heads in shame. They behaved like common hooligans. There is no place in society for hoodlums like these. They have brought shame on every decent pupil who attends this school.'

She went on to say that the incident was brought to her attention late yesterday afternoon and that she had already begun her own investigations, which, she added, were quite close to exposing the people involved. 'When I do eventually find who is reponsible, they will be expelled immediately from the school and my report will be sent to the police!'

The deputy head then took over centre stage and put his tuppence worth in. I looked along the row of kids sitting beside me. Many of the boys in my year were smiling. They and I knew what had really gone on at the sports day.

About twenty boys from the fourth year had arrived at Mostpur Park to watch the sports day. None of us were in school uniform and were all casually dressed. A group of kids from a grammar school in Wimbledon came along on bikes and, as the last one passed us, thinking he was a safe distance from us, he stopped and shouted, 'Wankers!' at us. We gave chase and, to our surprise and the horror of Big Mouth on the bike, we caught up with him. One of our chaps punched him in the mouth and pinched his bike from under his arse. We then gave chase to the rest of his pals, who had cycled up the road as fast as their legs would take them. The boy who was caught had to stand and watch as his bike was thrown over a fence. We walked off, laughing. Little Lord Fauntleroy and his chums had been given a bit of a thrashing by those common louts from the comprehensive.

As we walked away, I saw the kid retrieving his bike from the other side of the fence so I didn't see how he could claim it had been stolen.

After assembly I had a two-hour metalwork lesson and then it was time for a fifteen-minute break. We gathered in the playground and the talk was of the rumpus at the sports day. The minor skirmish had been blown out of all proportion.

'Fucking little grasses!' someone said. 'They started it, the toffee-nosed bastards. We never nicked that kid's bike.'

We all agreed it was handbags at twenty paces. Only one kid had copped a right-hander. Before the bell went to resume lessons we all agreed that if one of us was pulled up in front of the headmistress the rest of the boys would go to her office and explain what had happened. By the sound of her voice and the way she had acted, though, she had decided those involved were guilty before she'd heard all the facts. What happened to British justice and being innocent until proven guilty? That seemed to have been forgotten.

After a couple of weeks, the whole thing blew over. There was talk of a revenge attack and that the Old Bill knew the names of those involved and that they were being kept under surveillance by plain-clothes officers. It was more James Bond than Pollards Hill High. It was way over the top.

The main thing on my mind now was to try and find a job. I was due to leave school in a fortnight's time and I hadn't really given any thought to how I wanted to make my living. I'd seen the careers adviser at school but he gave the same old spiel to all the boys about staying on and getting A- or O-Levels, joining the army or learning a trade. I'd asked my dad if he could get me a start at his place. He worked as a maintenance fitter, so a job as a fitter's mate would have done me, but I don't think the old man was too keen to have me around him all day.

I trooped around every factory estate in the Mitcham area, but I was met with the same reply every time. There were jobs, but firms wanted people with experience or kids with qualifications. These were mundane, everyday jobs in factories. And what kid just leaving school with all sorts of A-levels coming out of his ears would take a dead-end shitty job like that? And as far as job experience went, how could I have job experience when I was just leaving school? The job centre and the dole queue, here I come.

Back at school on Monday I realised there were now only another five days until I was out of that shit hole. Back at the morning assembly, the headmistress made her usual grand entrance from the rear of the hall, marching down the aisle, along the front row and up the stairs that led to the stage. She looked furious. She pulled a piece of paper from her cardigan pocket, adjusted her glasses and started reading out a list of names: 'SMITH, BAKER, REID, READER, MARNEY, LEES, KING,' she said, and added a few more. When she came to the end of the list, she told everyone whose name was called to stand up. We got to our feet. I could feel my face going red as I sensed all eyes in the hall staring at us. 'What the fuck is this all about?' I wondered. 'Has someone grassed on us about the fight at the sports day?'

'Boys and girls, members of staff!' the headmistress said. 'The people now standing in front of you were identified by a member of my staff as being likely to cause trouble on the last day of term before the start of the summer holidays. These people were going to go out of their way to create disruption and cause havoc this Friday. Their plans included letting down the tyres on teachers' cars, letting off fire alarms, making water- and flour-bombs for use against myself and members of my staff. Well, their mindless plans have been rumbled. They were due to leave the school this Friday, but instead, as from this very moment, these mindless morons will be escorted off the school premises by the deputy headmaster. Those of you who have had your names called and are standing, please make your way to the back of the hall and leave by the fire exit. Would everyone else please remain seated.'

As we made our way out, a lot of the kids stood up and shook our hands and slapped our backs, much to the disgust of the head-mistress. 'Will the rest of the school please remain seated!' she shouted.

The boys who had been picked out stood in the playground chatting. None of us was really bothered, but we wanted to know who had grassed us up. The names of a few prefects were bandied about as likely candidates. It could be anyone, though: there were hundreds of crawl-arses looking to get in the headmistress's good books.

'Walk this way!' snapped the deputy head as he set off at a brisk pace towards the school gates. He had a slight limp, and following him was us lot, all of whom had suddenly developed the same kind of limp. It was quite comical to see a line of schoolboys taking the piss and the teacher not having a clue what was going on.

When we reached the large black gates he stopped and let us limp past him. I never did like that man. He seemed to detest children and was always cold and aloof.

'Keep off the school premises and don't come back!' he said as he turned and walked away. The rest of the teachers stood on the steps of the main entrance, watching. I bet some of them hated him as much as we did.

'Come out here and say that,' one of the lads yelled back at him.

'He won't come out,' said someone else. 'He's frightened one of us will drag him from the safety of the school grounds and beat the shit out of him. Don't worry yourself, we won't be coming back.'

We watched him limp back towards the school. He was met on the steps by the headmistress who no doubt thanked him for his bravery.

'That's it, boys, school's finished with, we're out in the big wide world!' I said. 'Now we've got to fend for ourselves.'

Not one of us had a job and, to tell you the truth, none of us seemed to be that bothered. I'd always grafted from the age of about ten. Apart from my paper rounds, I'd done waste-paper collecting and sold it to the paper mill. I'd washed cars. I'd washed people's windows. I'd run errands for fags, papers, wool and groceries for the old grunters who lived near me. I'd been out touting for scrap metal. So I knew I could make a living. I said farewell to the others and I wished them well for the future.

A couple of years before, the school I'd gone to in Western Road in Mitcham had closed down and so we'd had to choose another school to go to within the borough. My first choice had been Pollards Hill High and, along with nearly all my mates, I was accepted. The only trouble was that the new school was a twenty-minute bus ride away so on the first morning all the lads, not knowing what sort of welcome we would get, decided to meet up at the bus-stop so we could travel to the new school together. We need not have worried. The kids made us feel more than welcome, and since then most of us had become really good friends. Today was an example of that solidarity.

It wasn't until I was sitting upstairs on the bus all alone that I started to wonder what Mum would say when I got home. Should I tell her the truth? Would she go mad? Would she even care? I arrived home to an empty house and even the dog looked at me as if to say 'What you doing home at this time of day?'.

'Mind your own business,' I said and the dog rolled over and went back to sleep.

After a couple of hours of being bored and having no one to talk to, thousands of things were going through my head. Perhaps I should have paid more attention at school. Perhaps the teachers were right all along and I should have stayed on and got some qualifications. No, I wasn't having that.

Mum came in at lunchtime and didn't even ask what I was doing home at this time of day. The first thing she asked was could I run up to the corner shop and get her some fags, a loaf of bread and a pint of milk. What was this, the weekly shopping trip I was being sent out to do?

'No problem,' I said, trying to keep in her good books. I was there and back in five minutes and she was happily puffing away on a No. 6 fag.

'That's better!' she said. 'I've been on me feet all morning since six o'clock.'

I didn't know how she worked that out: she didn't get up until seven. Still, I wasn't arguing with her. I didn't want her asking me why I wasn't at school. If she asked I'd tell her they'd given me the rest of the week off to try and find a job. Yeah, that's what I'd tell her. I grabbed my jacket and told her I was off out to have a look for a job.

'Why's that, boy?' she asked.

'Well, I leave school this week, Mother, so I thought I might go out and find myself a job so that there's some more money coming into the house.'

'That'll be nice, boy,' she replied as she lit up another cigarette.

I walked around aimlessly for hours without any luck. The rest of the week was the same. I missed all my mates from school and I was bored silly being on my own.

On Saturday morning, my cousin Kevin phoned and asked if I'd like to stay at his place for the summer holidays. Kev was a year younger that me so he wasn't leaving school until this time the following year. He was right into tinkering with old cars and motorbikes, so when he left school he knew what he wanted to do for a living. From an early age Kev had wanted to be a grease monkey.

I accepted his offer to spend some time with him in the Surrey countryside where he and my auntie lived. I got all my gear together and carefully stuffed it into a holdall. Auntie Maise would iron it for me once I got there. I told Mum my plans and she agreed I should go and enjoy myself.

'My sister will look after you, boy,' she said, 'and anyway the break will help you decide what you want to do jobwise. I'll come down in a couple of weeks and Alan and I will bring you back in his car.' She pressed a ten-pound note into the palm of my hand. 'I'll tell your dad where you've gone,' she said as she waved me off.

'Cheers, Mum,' I said and gave her a peck on the cheek.

'Give my love to Aunt Maise!' she shouted as I headed off towards Wimbledon Station. From there I took the train to Frimley.

Kev met me off the train and we walked back to his house, which was on the edge of a wood. His mum and dad were divorced but Maise still lived in the house. It was a beautiful house, in a lovely street. There was even a lake at the bottom of the road. Kev's old man owned his own engineering business in London, and as well as this country pad he also had a forty-foot yacht. The house was based on a Swedish design with the bedrooms downstairs and the living-room and kitchen upstairs. It was a real nobs' area, and the neighbours included doctors, pilots and barristers, so I knew I would fit right in if any of them were to have a dinner or cocktail party.

Kev's old man spoilt him rotten. He had everything – the best clothes, a few quid in his pocket and a brand new Raleigh Chopper. His dad had even bought him a German Shepherd puppy which was grown up now but, as with everything, it wasn't long before Kev grew bored of it. He'd never really given it any attention. The poor thing was stuck in a fenced-off run in the back garden and was never taken out. That changed after a few days when the dog came with me every time I went over to the woods with Kev on our bikes. We used to spend hours there. One day we sat on the top of a hill and watched some soldiers from the local barracks playing war games. The sound of gunfire and bombs exploding and the different-coloured smoke drifting past us was unbelievable. It was really surprising to see that the common was frequently used by the army, and we'd often come across soldiers heavily camouflaged with blackened faces hiding in water-filled ditches. 'Perhaps I should join the army,' I thought to myself. 'They seem to have a good time.' But I knew I wouldn't be able to hack being away from home.

After a week of living the life of the country squire, I needed something lively to do. Kev told me about a disco on Saturday night at the Scout Hall in the town. 'Shall we go?' he asked. 'We might meet some birds.'

Just the mention of girls had me interested. I'd seen enough rabbits, foxes and badgers to last me a lifetime. 'Too right,' I said, 'let's go for it.'

The rest of the week was spent in brilliant sunshine, riding Kev's scrambling motorbike or cycling or walking the dog for miles through the woods. I was really enjoying myself and work was the last thing on my mind.

The disco on Saturday night started at eight o'clock. Kev and I decided to get there for dead on eight. When we arrived there was already a queue of thirty or forty people, mainly girls, waiting to get in. Kev spoke to one of the girls, who told him that the caretaker couldn't find the keys to unlock the door. She pointed towards a transit van and said the DJ was sitting inside waiting patiently for the hall to open so that he could set up his gear. We could hear activity coming from the hall and finally the lights came on. The smiling caretaker opened the front door and we all piled in. A scoutmaster-type bloke came round and asked everyone if they'd paid on the way in. A few dozy birds dug into their purses and handed over the entrance fee. He was getting fuck all from Kev and me. We told him we'd already paid.

Before long, the music and the flashing lights started up and the place was buzzing. Kev knew all the local girls and he introduced me to quite a few of them. 'This is my cousin Martin from London,' he'd tell them, and they'd look at me as if to say 'Where's London?' It was only half an hour on a train from Frimley, but to some of these girls it could have been the other side of the moon. I was the new kid on the block, chatting up the women and getting their attention. The boys didn't say anything but some of them did give me a bit of eyeball.

When 'The Funky Chicken' came on, I went into the well-rehearsed routine the boys and I had done at Merton Hall. I danced around like a chicken, my legs bending from side to side and my arms going up and down like I was trying to lay an egg. This dance didn't get a second look around my way – all the kids did it – but here they looked at me as if I was having an epileptic fit.

I had a couple of slow dances with one or two of the girls and made sure I rubbed my cory up against them as I held them tight and danced up close. One girl in particular stood out and when we danced I could tell she wanted what I wanted. Problem was, her boyfriend was watching our every move.

At the end of the evening Kev and I said goodnight to everyone and set off down the dark lanes that led to his house. The sound of bats screeching and owls hooting could be heard coming from the woods – a bit different from London, where girls screaming and glass breaking were the only sounds normally heard late at night.

The headlights of a car coming up the dirt track behind us made us step to one side and let it pass. It was doing a fair old speed as it whizzed down the lane.

'That's the girl you were nearly having sex with on the dance floor,' said Kev once it had passed, 'and that's her boyfriend driving. He's only come this way to show off his Cortina. He sometimes comes to the school and picks her up in his car.'

'How old is he?' I asked.

'Nineteen,' replied Kev.

'Fucking nineteen! What's a nineteen-year-old doing going out with a fifteen-year-old girl? Why ain't he knocking around with kids his own age?'

'He's a right scruffy bastard, a right soap-dodger, who stinks of BO. He's a bit of a halfwit, a sort of Neanderthal man. Not the full ticket,' said Kev.

He went on to tell me that the bloke was always playing about under the bonnet of his car, his face and hands permanently covered in dirt and grease and no matter how many times he washed his hands the dirt stayed under his fingernails. He lived with his mum and dad and eight brothers and sisters and their house was a right tip with bits of old cars lying in the front and back gardens and half the windows in the house boarded up. Worn-out car batteries and broken tellies lined the garden path to their front door. The family were known locally as the Munsters.

'Wonder what she sees in him,' I said to myself.

The following weeks were filled with sunshine and playing around on the Common. It was just fantastic. I swore to myself that if I ever came into money this was where I'd like to live. But to have money I'd first have to find a decent job and I wouldn't do that spending all my time lazing around in the Surrey countryside. I'd been down there for nearly six weeks and not seen my mum and dad in all that time. I'd spoken to Mum on the phone and she told me that she and my brother would be down to pick me up and take me home a week this Saturday.

'You've got to come home and find a job,' she said. 'Plus Maise must be sick of the sight of you.'

That evening Kev and I were wondering what to do. We were just kicking a ball up against the garage door and it must have been getting on Maise's nerves because she came out the house and yelled at us: 'Piss off somewhere else! The noise of that ball banging against the door is driving me bleedin' potty!'

Perhaps Mum was right and I had outstayed my welcome. Kev decided to walk down the road and see if his mate was at home. I couldn't be bothered and told him I'd wait outside and sit on the doorstep till he got back. After half an hour of waiting, I was getting very bored. I decided to have a ride around on his orange Chopper bike. I cycled down to the lake – and who was sitting there on a bench staring into the still murky waters but the girl from the disco. Her eyes were red and puffy and she was sobbing uncontrollably.

'You all right?' I asked. Without looking up, she told me to leave her alone. 'Sorry to disturb you,' I said and began to cycle off.

'Wait, Martin!' she called. 'I'm sorry, but it's that boyfriend of mine, he's so horrible to me. He treats me like shit. I've had enough.' I put the bike down and sat on the bench beside her. I gave her my handkerchief, and she blew her nose. She tried to hand it back to me; I told her to keep it.

'Don't get all upset,' I said. 'I'll tell you something – men just aren't worth it.'

She looked at me and smiled.

'That's why I'm not gay,' I went on, 'men are so horrible.'

She laughed. 'I feel so much better for seeing you,' she told me. 'How come you're on your own?'

I explained that Kevin had gone to his mate's and that I was just having a cycle around.

'Going anywhere in particular?' she asked.

'I might have a ride over the woods.'

'Well, I'll come with you,' she said, so I moved along the saddle and she climbed on the back of the bike and held on to me as I pedalled off. We talked about the disco down at the Scout Hall and she told me how much she had wished she could have ended up with me that night. She said she had seen me and Kev walking home and that she felt like telling her boyfriend to stop the car so that she could get out and go home with me. 'When I got to his house, we had sex together and I imagined it was you making love to me,' she finished.

'Fucking hell!' I thought to myself, 'I've struck gold here! If this bird don't want a portion of cory, then I'm a monkey's uncle!'

I stopped the bike and turned around and kissed her. She responded by sticking her tongue down my throat. We got off the bike and lay down on the ground in the middle of the woods. She put her hand down my trousers and fished my dick out of my pants. Without even thinking, I pulled her knickers off and pushed my prick deep inside her. I undid her bra and felt her big round tits. I lasted all of a minute pumping up and down before I came my lot, pulling it out and shooting all over her belly.

I pulled my trousers and pants up and watched as she lay on the ground and wriggled back into her knickers. She brushed the twigs and leaves off her skirt and she refastened her bra. She stood up and gave herself another brush down and we were back on the bike together and heading for home.

'Drop me off back at my house,' was all she said. The rest of the journey was done in complete silence. Just before we reached her house, I spotted her boyfriend sitting outside in his Cortina. 'Stop here!' she said and climbed off the back of the bike. She leant forward and gave me peck on the cheek. 'Thanks for being so understanding,' she whispered. I watched her walk over and climb into the front seat of his car and they zoomed off.

I cycled back to Kevin's and found him sitting in the front garden with his mate Keith, fiddling with an old motorbike. His hands and face were covered in oil.

'Where have you been?' he asked me

'Wouldn't you like to know,' I said. Even if I was to tell him, I'm sure he wouldn't believe me, and if he did, he would start sniffing around her himself.

The following morning I got up bright and early and Kev and I were stuck for things to do. The football season was only a couple of weeks old and I hadn't been to a game yet, so I looked down the fixtures to see who was playing. I noticed Aldershot were at home to Brentford and, seeing as Aldershot was only ten minutes up the road, we decided to go along and watch the game.

We arrived just as the match was about to kick off. The Aldershot stadium was like nothing I'd ever seen before. It must have been the only ground in the country that had a three-foot-high fence round it that was meant to stop you getting in for nothing. I should imagine more people bunked in than paid at the turnstiles. It was a funny little ground with most of the spectators crowded under the covered terrace opposite where we'd just bunked in. By the looks of it and by the sound of it, both Aldershot and Brentford fans were standing side by side.

We walked along the terraces and stood in amongst the Aldershot fans. Kev spoke to a couple of kids who went to his school. They told him there was a mob of Brentford skinheads about a hundred-strong at the back of the terrace. They had the Old Bill keeping a close eye on them, so there had been no trouble yet. The two mobs were trying to out-shout and out-sing one another as they gave their support to their team.

We walked up to the back and had a look at the Brentford mob. Sure enough, they had the Old Bill with them. I was an old hand by now at sussing out opposing mobs. My years of following Chelsea had served me well. I'd listened and learned and I was terrace-wise as well as street-wise. We stood right next to them and they stared over at us. A kid about my age with a Brentford scarf on felt safe standing next to the police, so he started getting mouthy and singled me out.

'Where's your mob, you Aldershot tosser? We're in your end, boys, what you going to do about it?' he taunted and jeered and gave the wankers sign.

I told him that he was not in my team's end, as my team, Chelsea, were playing away up north. He thought about this for a few seconds and then asked why a Chelsea supporter would be at an Aldershot versus Brentford game.

'I'm here on holiday,' I told him and moved through the Old Bill lines to stand next to him. This unnerved him a bit and he wasn't quite sure how to deal with me close up. He was a bit fidgety. The coppers were watching us, ready to pounce at the first sign of trouble.

'Having a nice holiday, are you?' he asked, not really knowing what to say.

'Yeah, not bad,' I replied. 'I always come to Aldershot for my summer holidays. I used to go with the family to Spain or Greece, but now I always come to Aldershot. I think it's them nice army boys in their uniforms that makes me come back every year.'

He'd heard enough and quickly walked away down the terraces. Me making out I was a shirtlifter had frightened the life out of him. I saw him stop and tell a group of lads about me, pointing up the terrace towards where I was standing. I blew a kiss down to them and then walked off into the crowd. I seemed to have upset him and his mates. They'd been spooked by one bloke on his own whom they thought was gay. It didn't take a lot to have Brentford boys on their toes.

After the game we headed back to Kev's. As we approached his house, I spotted my brother's car parked outside. It looked like it was jam-packed with all sorts of gear – suitcases, vases, lampshades, rugs, old clothes and records were all loaded on the back seat and in the front. My mum and brother came out of the house to greet me. She hadn't seen me for a long time and she smothered me in red lipstick. 'How's my baby been?' asked Mum, giving me a bear hug that squeezed every breath of air out of my lungs.

'He's been fine,' said Maise, 'he ain't been one bit of trouble.'

'What's all the gear in the motor?' I asked

'Me and your brother came down to pick you up and Maise told me you and Kev had gone to football, so we went to a local jumble sale and picked up a few bargains!'

'Very nice,' I said, 'but you're a week early. I thought I was going home next weekend.'

'That's all changed. Your dad's got you a job at his works and you can start Monday.'

'Fucking hell, I don't believe it!' I kissed everyone. I was well pleased. I grabbed my belongings and squeezed into the back seat of the car. I wound the window down and thanked Maise and Kev for having me.

Alan and Mum got in and we chugged off up the road. The car was so full up the back axle was nearly resting on the ground. Clouds of black smoke bellowed from the exhaust. All I wanted to talk about was the job with Dad and what it would entail.

'Wait until you get home,' said Mum, trying to shut me up. 'Your dad will know more about it than me.'

I even knew what I was going to spend my first week's wages on. I'd get my wage packet and spend every penny on clothes. I was going to blow the lot. After that, I'd put a few pounds a week away and save up for a car – nothing too flash, maybe a Cortina or a Capri, or an Anglia or a little old banger, just as a runaround. I might even go for leopardskin covers on the seats. I don't know if it was the excitement or the funny-smelling fag my brother was smoking, but it wasn't long before I crashed out, fast asleep. My dreams soon turned from owning and driving a Cortina to driving along the King's Road in a convertible Rolls-Royce with two blonde dollybirds by my side.

This first job was just a stepping-stone to better things. School was now behind me, and making a few quid from work and living well was my new ambition, but could I succeed?

Epilogue

One of the characters in this book, Mickey Greenaway, sadly passed away in August of last year. Mick was well known to almost everyone over at Stamford Bridge, to the lot of us that followed Chelsea and, more importantly, we knew Mick in his role as the leader of the Chelsea shed during the 1960s and '70s. We have many fond memories of him, his zigger-zagger chant would drift across the terraces at nearly every ground in the country wherever Chelsea would find themselves playing. Mick was the team's number-one fan, he was Mr Chelsea. In his latter years, and with the changing face of type of fan that flocked to Stamford Bridge, Mick was rarely seen at football. He did leave the supporters with the song 'One Man Went to Mow' and it is still sung to this day. With Chelsea not winning a trophy for nearly 25 years, the success in the silverware department recently must have brought a smile to Mick's face. Rumour has it the Ken Bates, the Chelsea chairman, is even going to name a bar in the new west stand after Mick. I hope so; it would be a fitting tribute to a man who followed the Blues thru thick and thin. It would also show that Ken Bates does appreciate the role played by the supporters in our great and famous club.

God bless you Mick, you are sadly missed.